MW00635068

The Lightworker's Guide to Grounding Energy

Amy Scott Grant
Terry Robnett, RN

Liberto Press
Castle Rock, CO

Published by Liberto Press
Castle Rock, Colorado, USA
© 2018 Amy Scott Grant and Terry Robnett
Book cover, design, and production by LibertoPress.com
Photograph of Amy Scott Grant by Andrew E. Grant
Photograph of Terry Robnett, RN by Tamara Muñoz

Although the authors and publisher have made every effort to ensure that the information in this book was correct at press time, the authors and publisher do not assume and hereby disclaim any liability to any party for any loss, damage, or disruption caused by errors or omissions, whether such errors or omissions result from negligence, accident, or any other cause. Please remember to drink plenty of water when performing or receiving any kind of energy work or healing.

ISBN: 978-0-9974466-4-7

First Liberto Press printing, October 2018

Dedication

This book is dedicated to Mother Gaia.

Thank you for remaining ever steady
and for grounding us, always.

Table of Contents

I Am Grounded

By Cheri Hayashi

Out in the meadow
Warm wind on my face
Roots sprout from my soles
Stretching into place

Arms spread wide open
Morph into a tree
A beautiful oak
Grace for all to see

Strong and sturdy trunk
Branches so buoyant
The crown full and lush
Leaves smooth and vibrant

A feeling of peace
Washes over me
Oneness with the Earth
Pure tranquility

Introduction

Welcome to the second book in the "Lightworker's Guide" series by Amy Scott Grant and Terry Robnett. By the time you finish reading this book, you will not only feel more grounded, but you will also possess many powerful tools in your arsenal to help you ground your own energy, spaces, projects, things, and the energy of those around you. Grounding or "earthing" energy will help you feel more confident, more relaxed, more centered, and better equipped to handle whatever curve balls life throws your way.

We (Amy and Terry) will share with you numerous ways to ground energy, and we encourage you to try them all! Please feel free to keep what resonates with you and leave the rest. We have also invited some fellow Lightworkers to share their insights and experiences with you, and you'll find these contributions in italics throughout each chapter. At the end of each chapter, you'll find a few "Food for Thought" questions to help you explore and clarify what you've learned as it applies specifically to you and your current stage of your Lightworker's journey. At the end of this book, you'll find a glossary of terms as well as more information about the authors.

You can also hang out with us and a number of very cool like-minded peeps (from beginners to advanced) in our private Lightworker's Guide community:

TheLightworkersGuide.com

With love, light, and badassery,

Amy & Terry

Chapter 1:

What Is Grounding?

"And you, young lady, are grounded!" Remember all the naughty things we did when we were kids? How about those times when you actually got caught and got grounded by the parental units, remember that?

Parents use the phrase "ground" to refer to a form of discipline or consequence where the child is not allowed to go out or do anything fun. No phones or devices, no screen time, no social media, no ratting around the mall with friends, no trips to the movies, no playing in the neighborhood, no car, no pedaling like the wind, no school dances, no dates, no fun! As kids, we came to associate the phrase "being grounded" with all things negative: punishment for our transgressions and no fun whatsoever.

"Grounded" has an equally unpleasant meaning for travelers who are anxious to reach their destination but have been delayed due to their plane being "grounded" and unable to fly. Again, no fun.

But, as adults on a daily quest for enlightenment, grounding has an entirely different meaning.

Okay, It's Not a Punishment. So What Is It?

Grounding is a word that refers to the process of becoming grounded. And grounded simply means **being centered or well balanced.** In metaphysical and energy terms, **to ground** means to connect to the earth and benefit from its steady, stable energy.

Consider this sentence: "I watched my sister's boys while she was out of town. One of them was scattered and all over the place, but the other one seemed well-grounded."

Did your mind form an image of the two boys? What sorts of words would you use to describe what you imagined about the well-grounded boy?

Feeling grounded could be described as:

> Calm
> Centered
> Balanced
> Peaceful
> Sensible
> Connected
> Stable
> Relaxed
> Reliable
> Capable
> Both feet planted firmly on the ground

Why Ground?

Electrical grounding (usually shortened to "grounding" or "earthing," as our European friends say) is a direct or indirect method by which a device is connected to the earth for a variety of reasons. Originally, grounding was performed to help prevent accidental shock or injury, but since the early days of the invention of various electronics, many additional benefits have been discovered. Grounding provides a zero-potential reference point for voltage, eliminates electrostatic buildup, minimizes lightning damage, drains off any undesirable buildup of electrical charge, and helps electrical devices maintain a steady voltage.

This effect is mirrored in humans thanks to the effect of energy grounding. When grounded and connected to stable earth energy, excess anxiety or overwhelm is siphoned off of you and into the earth. The benefits are plentiful: shock is reduced, the brain operates more effectively, the emotions are more stable, and you are less affected by (lightning) outbursts, surges of energy, or unexpected turns of events.

Sarah A. Sherman: Earth Me, Please

Ground, just the very word evokes the earth – breathtaking, stable, and ever present. Our feet walk on it every day. Our very beings are created from what it is made out of. Kindled in the souls of our parents and breathed into existence by the breath of the creator, we were called to be here standing on its surface today. Drinking the water that nourishes us and keeps our body fluid and supple, helping to discharge toxins. Eating the gifts of food it gives us—the plants, the fruits, the seeds, the nuts. Each breath we take is the very presence of the creator in our life, as we breathe this song of our lives together.

Ground. Stable, strong in the present moment. Ground. Take a moment and pause. Are you here in the now? Listen to your mind, feel with your heart… are you present? Are you in a timeless sense of centered stability, no matter where you are at? Or are you on the freeway and late for the next meeting with 1,000 things happening, seemingly all at one time?

Separate the moment and free your mind, steady your soul. Feel the mother earth at your feet, take three deep breaths, and clear your mind. Close your eyes and breathe and breathe again. Connect with gratitude in each breath and breathe with God... the breath is the sign of life. Connect within your heart replacing all with this peace, this thankfulness. Feel the gratitude move through your being. Go to the crown of your head and run the gratitude down through your body directly into the Earth. Connect with the earth in gratitude. Lift your hands above your head and bend forward touching your hands on the ground. Repeat until you are in your center. Sometimes in your center, you can repeat for a long, long, time.

Why Is Grounding Important for Lightworkers?

Webster's Dictionary defines "Lightworker" as—oh wait, that's right. It doesn't define it at all, because "Lightworker" is not *in* the dictionary. And yet, the term is fairly commonplace among all walks of energy workers and nontraditional healers. Put simply, *a Lightworker is one who works with energy toward a positive end.*

If that sounds a bit vague or generalized, think about it this way. How would you define "food"? Perhaps: "a substance one eats." That short and sweet phrase defines this broad term, but without going into the finer details of the difference between pizza and chocolate soufflé, and without naming all the different styles and nationalities of food, or how to balance flavors, or how to cook. Lightworking is as vast and varied as food, and in many cases, just as enjoyable. If you wish to learn more about the different types and skillsets of Lightworkers, get yourself a copy of *The Lightworker's Guide to Getting Started.*

Lightworkers will find it especially important to ground energy, lest we get swept away in the massive energy shifts that surround us. No matter what kind of Lightworking you're partial to, on any given day, your energy work with yourself or others could cause you to be subjected to such delights as:

- negative entities
- energy portals
- past life issues such as betrayals and/or unresolved conflicts
- toxic energy
- physical illnesses and conditions
- cords of energy
- old energetic wounds
- energy vampires
- strong emotions running rampant
- and much more

These are of particular concern if you are a Lightworker who is also an empath or a highly sensitive person (HSP), as it means you would be more likely to personally experience the effects of such cosmic dregs.

Have you ever felt the energy in the room change when a certain person walked into the space? Have you yourself ever felt your own energy downshift when you were in the presence of a very toxic individual, or a person who was visibly upset? Yes, we've been there, too. It ain't pretty!

As professional Lightworkers, we actively choose to help individuals with their energy healing, which means we will almost certainly encounter many if not all of the unsavory items on the above list. Learning to ground your energy will help you avoid taking on these negative energies as you heal others from them. Lightworkers also benefit greatly from being able to ground their spaces, their businesses, their household, their clients, their electronics, their family members, and anything else deemed important.

Violetta Pleshakova: Earthing for Divine Humans

For the dominant part of my decade's worth of lightworking, I struggled with grounding.

And when I say struggled, I mean a whole spectrum of challenges, ranging from feeling perpetually spaced out to experiencing bone-deep resistance to the very fact of being alive. Why would I be in denial of something so essential as connection with the planet I am incarnated on? That's the question I kept asking myself.

As a young girl, I was in love with nature and spent my formative years roaming around the Russian countryside, having past life flashbacks, and sensing undercurrents of energy. I was not of this world—and at the same time miraculously one with it.

That effortless state of being psychically open yet naturally connected to everything faded away as I succumbed to adult pressures of belonging and becoming. Deep within, I was still craving that unity.

No amount of salt baths, barefoot walking, or holding on to black tourmaline for dear life made a difference until I dared to unveil—and heal—the root of my resistance to the earthly plane. I inquired into the pain that powered it, and confronted a mesmerizing juxtaposition: total devotion to my Soul's purpose co-existed with gripping fear of actually living it. My quarrel was not with Earth, it was with my reservations about showing up on it and for it. In the effort to preserve my Soul's divine spark, I renounced its human counterpart. And that made me feel like a fraud. I realized I could be truly of service in this world only if I was fully grounded and embodied in it.

10

Hit hard by this revelation, I decided to follow the trail of childhood memories and explore finding my ground again through the pure vibrations of nature.

One particularly rough day I gravitated to a park and surrendered to my exhaustion. I lay down on bare ground, and for once, allowed myself to just be held.

Then, I felt Her—Gaia, the Earth Spirit, the Planetary Mother.

She was so naked, so available and willing to receive ALL of me: my self-hatred and disdain, entitlement and despair. She was willing to hold it all, and asked nothing back. The force of her radical receptivity and the unconditionality of her compassion cracked me open to Love.

Through being in Her immediate, immanent presence, I started reconciling my Soul and body. Breath by breath, I mothered my spirit back into my physicality. Bit by bit, I embraced my rawness, realness, humanness.

What started off as a tentative exploration, gradually developed into a deep, heartfelt communion. Willingness was the key, and the finality of my choice to be alive sealed the deal.

If I as a Soul chose to be here, now, on this planet—I choose to be here unapologetically, incorruptibly, fully. No back doors. I am all IN, and I can have it all: the above, the below, and everything in between.

This is my path of devotion to the sacred alchemy of the mundane and the magical.

This is me, a Soul in a body.

Soulfully sensual, heavenly grounded, divinely human.

When Should You Ground?

Any time is a good time to ground. While standing in line at the post office, sitting in traffic, enjoying a long soak, talking to your teenager, or meeting your future in-laws for the first time. Plus any other time you want to feel stable, calm, and relaxed.

As a general rule, it's best to ground preventatively, and we'll look at some passive ways to do that in a bit. However, you can actively ground in the middle of a crisis, provided you can remember to do so.

Grounding can literally be done any time, any place. In fact, there are methods by which you can ground yourself automatically, 24/7.

In this book, we will dive into a number of ways to ground, and we will further explore passive methods, active methods, and combination methods. We'll even show you how to create your own grounding tools and techniques.

If you're not feeling calmer, steadier, and more stable by the end of this book, then you're not trying. Seriously. Grounding is so quick and easy that even a very young child can do it. In fact, children often ground themselves quite naturally, and as you continue reading through this book, you may realize that you used to do some of these very things when you were a child!

Terry Robnett: Buried

Born, raised, and living in Southern California, I have always been a hop, skip, and a jump from many beaches. I used to love love love going to the beach! I spent countless happy summers living on the beaches of San Diego, Malibu,

Carpinteria, Newport, Santa Barbara, and Santa Monica (just to name a few). It has always been my haven.

I had a certain routine every time I went. I would literally live in the water all day until I got all pruney, or my fingers and toes went numb. After finally getting out of the water, I would bury my whole body in the warm sand. It always made me feel like I was melting into the ground and becoming one with it. I remember it very vividly like it was yesterday and how it felt SO amazing. First, I would make a pillow out of sand to lay my head on and then proceed to carve out a shallow space large enough to submerge my whole body. I would then cover the rest of my body with all the sand I carved out and just lay there for a while until I felt it was time to get up. I am unable to explain it, but there was something extremely comforting and embracing about it. I feel that instinctively I knew this was something my mind, body, and soul needed.

I look back now as a grown adult with a lifetime of wisdom and experience and realize that it was literally like a cleansing and a re-centering. A pure form of grounding and refueling my whole being.

How Do You Know If You Need to Ground?

Fortunately, knowing when to ground is not like falling in love. It's not some inexplicable "you just know" kind of feeling. There are clear and specific signs that warn you it's time to ground.

How can you tell if you're not grounded? Here are a few indicators:

- Feeling overwhelmed
- Feeling like you can't settle down or sit still
- Feeling like you can't focus or concentrate

- Feeling like a lot of stuff is coming at you and you're not sure what to address first
- Feeling spaced out or flaky
- Feeling upset or experiencing any strong unpleasant emotion
- Feeling stressed out, maxed out, or tapped out
- Feeling off-balance, like you're not centered
- Feeling unsafe
- Feeling threatened
- Feeling like your head is in the clouds
- Getting a headache after being around other people or crowds
- Feeling like you need a minute to think, some quiet, or some time to yourself, *pronto*

Like many signs we receive from our bodies and our internal energy systems, the signs start out rather subtle, and will grow rapidly if ignored, in an increasingly intense attempt to gain your attention. Here's an example of how being ungrounded can escalate into a most unpleasant experience.

For example, let's say you're attending a party or social gathering and you don't expect to know many of the people in attendance. Just before the event, you might have some slightly uncomfortable **physical symptoms,** such as butterflies in your stomach, or feeling a bit fidgety. You could have some **emotional symptoms,** such as feeling a bit nervous or edgy. You may even have some **mental symptoms,** like pre-stressing over who might be there or what you should talk about or what you'll do if you don't know anyone there. You might fret over what you'll wear or how you'll look, or you might be pre-planning your escape just in case things get uncomfortable and you want to bolt.

If you stop and take a few moments to ground, you'll find that all of the above settles down, and you'll feel much calmer about attending. You might even look forward to the event, or feel excited.

However, if you do not ground, these symptoms are likely to grow. For example, they could lead to any or all of the following moderately uncomfortable experiences:

- **Physical symptoms,** such as eye twitching, nausea, sweating, clammy hands, feeling excessively warm, heart racing, inability to sit still/stand still, stammering, etc.
- **Emotional symptoms,** such as anxiety, fear, worry, nervousness, irritability, sadness, frustration, shutting down emotionally, putting up walls, stuffing your face as a way to avoid engaging in conversation, withdrawing by stepping outside, sitting in a corner, getting engrossed in your phone, etc.
- **Mental signs that manifest as physical actions,** such as avoiding eye contact, watching the clock, biting your nails or chewing your lip, bumping into people or things, sitting in the corner, shifting weight from foot to foot, inability to focus on the person talking to you, inability to speak clearly and cohesively, thinking of excuses why you have to leave, plotting your escape, etc.

At this point, there's so much chaos going on inside of you, grounding is likely the farthest thing from your mind. However, if you could shift gears long enough to ground, you would swiftly be able to resolve or at least diminish these experiences. But if you do not ground at this point, your situation could progress into full-blown panic, causing you to create an embarrassing scene or quickly and awkwardly leave the event. All of this can occur within a matter of minutes, or over a few hours, but without grounding, this is a very real potential scenario.

If it sounds like we're exaggerating, then you have likely never experienced any degree of social anxiety. In which case, the following example may provide a more relevant context for you.

Imagine you are walking in an unfamiliar city after dark, and you've lost your way. Nope, you don't have strong enough cell service to use a walking GPS app.

Initially, you may experience:

- Slightly uncomfortable **physical symptoms,** such as butterflies in your stomach, feeling fidgety, or paying closer attention to your surroundings.
- **Emotional symptoms,** feeling nervous or wary.
- **Mental symptoms,** like trying to recall the address where you're staying, or searching for anything that seems familiar, or a friendly face that might be able to direct you. You might be mentally counting the cash in your pocket, or deciding whether or not to hail a cab.

In this moment, you could ground, which would help you to feel safer, instantly. This would also give you more clarity, so you can figure out the best way to get to where you need to go. But if you don't ground, the fear will grow, likely leading to moderately uncomfortable feelings, for example:

- **Physical symptoms,** such as a stone in the pit of your stomach, sweating, clammy hands, shallow breathing, feeling excessively warm, heart racing, etc.
- **Emotional symptoms,** such as anxiety, fear, worry, nervousness, irritability that might appear as being mad at yourself for getting lost in the first place, sadness, frustration, despair, etc.
- **Mental signs that manifest as physical actions,** such as avoiding eye contact, glancing over your shoulder,

warily evaluating each person you pass on the street, chewing your lip, pulling your coat closer around you or putting your hand firmly on your wallet or purse, recalling horror stories from the news or television shows, fearing the worst, planning your escape, etc.

As with the social anxiety example, fear of being lost in an unfamiliar city can quickly devolve into panic without swift and immediate grounding. And far more dangerous than simply exiting a party without grace, your fear of the unknown (combined with a very active imagination) creates a strong attachment to a negative outcome: a powerful magnet for danger. An intervention of grounding at any point in this process can resolve your fears and put you in a more relaxed and solution-based frame of mind.

Consider that these are merely two examples, but that the need for grounding and the physical, emotional, and mental signs can be similarly identified for any life situation, such as:

- Preparing for a job interview
- Meeting your future in-laws
- Going on a first date
- Making a significant investment
- Shopping
- Buying a car
- Buying a house
- Making any major purchase
- Flying in an airplane
- Having sex
- Starting a new job
- Meeting a new client
- A sales call
- Starting a new eating plan or exercise program
- Public speaking
- Having a difficult conversation

- Breaking a commitment
- Breaking up with someone
- Having a baby
- Adopting a child
- Being a parent
- Interviewing someone
- Being interviewed
- Writing a book
- Launching a product
- Starting a business
- Closing a business
- Getting bad news
- Getting bad reviews
- Performing in any capacity
- Trying out a new look
- Changing your hairstyle
- Being around a person with a strong personality
- Being around someone who is negative, toxic, or an energetic drain
- Talking to your boss
- Talking to your neighbor
- Talking to a stranger
- Asking for help
- Traveling
- Traveling alone
- Traveling with kids
- Visiting a city for the first time
- Playing a new sport
- Taking lessons
- Giving lessons
- Trying anything new
- Being on Facebook or any social media
- Driving in traffic
- Driving in an unfamiliar area
- Etc.

Hopefully by now, you are starting to see the power of grounding and how it can be helpful in nearly every aspect of your life. The physical, emotional, and mental symptoms may vary slightly from situation to situation, but once you start to pay attention, you will quickly notice when grounding is warranted. As a by-product, you will also start to notice when someone around you isn't grounded. Whether or not you say anything about it is up to you, and that's something we'll cover later in this book.

How Do You Know if the Grounding Worked?

You'll know the grounding worked because you'll feel better instantly. Seriously, grounding works better than a glass of wine and without the calories. It's better than a shot, better than a nap, better than a pill, and better than anything you've ever used in the past to help you chillax. It's free, apart from whatever you spent on this delightfully informative and entertaining book. Totally worth it, by the way. In fact, why not buy a copy for a friend? Grounding is quick, it's easy, it's 100% portable, and it works, period.

After successfully grounding, you'll feel calmer, more centered, relaxed, and better equipped to deal with whatever situation is at hand. That's not to say that you can just ground once in the midst of total chaos and be done with it. Depending on how you're built, you may have to ground several times during a short span of time for full effect. Which brings us to the next point:

When It Comes to Grounding, We Are Not Created Equal

Are you familiar with Human Design? If not, we highly recommend that you check it out. Human Design is by far the most accurate "all about you chart" we have personally ever seen, and we have seen a lot of these. Every time something new comes along in the world of energy, people beg us to check it out, and we usually don't. We get our information and tools straight from Source, so we don't like to muddy the waters with a bunch of other people's methods and processes.

However, a friend and colleague of Amy's was so insistent that she look into it, that she arranged for Amy to have a private Human Design session with Burry Foss at no charge. Amy was so blown away by its remarkable accuracy and specificity that she soon insisted that all of her private and top tier clients have their charts read and shared with her before beginning any Spiritual Ass Kicker mentoring package. This was around the same time that Terry had decided to work with Amy, so of course, she also had a Human Design session with Burry and was impressed with the degree of detail provided. Incidentally, before *The Lightworker's Guide to Getting Started* book launched, we asked Burry to do a composite reading of our two charts. Imagine the validation we felt to discover our charts were perfectly aligned, that together we completed several key attributes for business, and that we balanced each other's strengths and weaknesses beautifully! It was a clear green light from the Universe to launch this book series and everything associated with it!

Understanding our Human Design and that of our clients has shaved hours—months, in some cases—off our healing time by providing laser-sharp insights and accuracy. If you want to have your chart read by the one person we recommend for this work, and enjoy a sweet discount, too, visit this link:

http://askamyanything.com/humandesign

Why are we telling you about this right now? Because when it comes to grounding, we are not all created equal, and one glance at your Human Design chart will tell us which camp you fall into:

Naturally Grounded vs. Not Naturally Grounded

Terry Robnett: Barefooted Bliss

As I reflect on my life, I take notice of how and when I intuitively knew how to ground. It came so quickly and easily to me as it all began as a baby/toddler. In fact, I believe this to be true for everyone. As a youngster, all of us intuitively know that by simply exposing our bare feet and walking around like that all day connected us to BLISS! A sense of FREEDOM! Right? Were you that kid who grew up living the majority of your life in bare feet? I for sure did! Heck, I was hiking in the mountains and ran the streets in my bare feet.

Now I know that at some point, there came a time throughout the journey when all that changed for most of us, but there are still people who absolutely cannot stand wearing shoes. The rest of us have just caved in to the world's conditioning over the need to protect our precious feet over the years. HELL, we only get one pair, right? At least that's what we were always told.

So, I encourage you (often) to close your eyes, relax for a minute, and let yourself go back to the time when you were barefoot and fancy-free. Remember how good, liberated, and happy you felt? Remember the freedom that it brought you? Remember how connected, powerful, and confident you felt? I am sure you can agree that by simply being in bare feet, grounding is a natural occurring event that requires no thought or exertion on your part. So how 'bout you kick off your shoes every chance you get and let those dogs loose to run wild and free?

Who Is Naturally Grounded?

Those of us who are naturally grounded, such as Terry and Amy, have a defined root chakra according to Human Design. Unless we are under stress or duress, we are usually grounded. Once we ground ourselves, we tend to stay grounded until something causes us to become ungrounded. It's the same principle as inertia. In many cases, we ground naturally and effortlessly, without conscious thought or effort. We are also likely to serve as a grounding force for others, and in some cases, we ground the entire space around us, simply by being present in the space itself.

If you haven't yet had your Human Design explained to you, how can you tell if you're naturally grounded? Here are a few clues:

- You don't tend to fly off the handle or come unglued unless something major happens.

- You typically keep a level head when things go wrong or when others around you are upset.

- Other people feel calmer in your presence.

Who Is Not Naturally Grounded?

If your Human Design shows you have an undefined root, you are most likely not naturally grounded. This isn't necessarily a bad thing, it just means you must be more consciously aware of your current state, and you would be wise to ground yourself often. Fortunately, there are many ways to ground, and some ways are very passive in nature. If you are not naturally grounded, you may experience some of the following:

- You often feel tired, can become overwhelmed easily, or lose your train of thought.
- Once you become stressed or spend time with someone negative, it can take awhile to feel like you're back on track.
- You often misplace items and forget appointments or other important stuff.

If you have taught yourself how to ground often, you may not have the experiences above, even if you're not a naturally grounded person. Likewise, if you are not naturally grounded, but your spouse or partner is, you may find the above experiences to be less predominant or even nonexistent in your life. This is because those who are not naturally grounded tend to feel safer and calmer in the presence of a very grounded person they know and trust.

Which is better? To be naturally grounded or not naturally grounded? One is not better than the other; it is simply important to understand which one pertains to you so that you can personally relate to what you learn in the rest of this book.

Heidi Cole: Living in My Head

I am quite often living life in my head. The first few times I had Reiki treatments, I could feel the energy of the thoughts as the Reiki energy flowed. It felt and sounded like white noise from a television left on past the end of the broadcast day. Does that even happen since cable took over? I rarely took time to ground as I was sooooo busy trying to stay busy so I could not work on my issues. If my life were a TV show, you wouldn't be able to see it because the antenna would be broken and hanging from the eaves, leaving you with, you guessed it, a snowy TV and the distinct wish for a little clarity.

Now as I look back to my past, the most grounded times I can remember revolve around light of some sort. In a way, it's sort of grounding AND enlightening at the same time.

My earliest recollections always involve Christmas tree lights. I would lay down under the tree, squint my eyes and look up at the Christmas lights, which left me feeling serene in my body and yet uplifted. The rainbow of lights would turn into stars by closing my eyes slightly, which seemed so appropriate for the season. Lying like this, I could dream about the gifts I wanted and feel the excitement building for the upcoming visit from Santa.

Another memory I have is sitting cross-legged in a beam of sunlight, eyes closed, watching images form on the back of my eyelids. Just sitting and enjoying the warmth of the sun. It wasn't so much a procedure of figuring out how to come back to my body but just enjoying the feeling of fully being in my body or maybe it was just being "a body" and not so much "a mind."

Occasionally, I get stuck living in my head, but when I feel like I need that stability and emotional calm, I tend to dream a little. I am in a lush forest with green leaves and vines dripping from the trees around the most beautiful and elaborate wooden throne. I walk past a small stream and climb the few steps to take my seat on the mossy throne. The seat is firm and supporting but soft and comfortable. I sink into the throne and allow it to support me. My feet are planted on the earth and my gaze softens. I encourage any anxious energy to leave through my legs and breathe in white light or love or peace or whatever my intention is. Then I continue with the task at hand....

As you continue reading, if you are naturally grounded, you will notice certain grounding methods that you already employ on a regular basis, as well as learning some new ones. If you are not naturally grounded, pay close attention to the passive grounding methods as well as the active ones, as you will likely need to utilize a combination of methods to successfully ground, especially if you do not currently live with someone who is naturally grounded.

Lightworker, Ground Thyself

Even the best, most experienced Lightworkers among us can become ungrounded from time to time. Besides the fact that

24

many Lightworkers are empaths who are more likely to pick up strong unpleasant emotions and/or physical feelings, *and* that in our line of work we often encounter many of the unpleasant things listed earlier in this chapter, there's also the fact that we often work in the realms outside of Mother Earth.

Many Lightworkers are operating in the upper chakras, relying on our crown, third eye, throat, and heart chakras, as we conduct our Lightworking duties. And while these upper chakras help us immensely to see, to feel, to know, and to heal, it is vital that we return to our lower chakras of root, sacrum, and solar plexus to restore our entire being into balance. There's nothing wrong with surfing energy in the ethers, as long as you return home to plant both feet on the ground.

New or inexperienced Lightworkers may also make the mistake of inadvertently taking on or picking up that which they are healing for others. In our efforts to heal another and reduce or resolve their suffering, we may unknowingly take that pain or adverse energy from them, thereby holding it in our own field. In Chapter 6, we'll explore specific grounding recommendations for Lightworkers, but for now, consider this: by grounding your energy before, during, and after a healing session, you will feel calmer and steadier, you will be able to confidently complete any reading or healing work, and you will be more readily able to recognize that which doesn't belong to you. Put simply, stay grounded so you don't take on shizzle that isn't yours. Likewise, the more grounded you are, the more your clients and students will be put at ease to address their own energy and healing. Not to mention the more stability you'll have around your finances, should you choose to make Lightworking your profession.

Now before we get specific and dive into a range of grounding methods in Chapter 2, take a few moments now to complete these Food for Thought questions.

Chapter 1 Food for Thought: nom nom nom

1. What words, thoughts, or feelings come to mind when you think about "grounding"?

2. Who or what in your life currently makes you feel ungrounded?

3. Based on what you've read in this chapter, do you think you are naturally grounded or not naturally grounded? If you already know because you've had your Human Design reading done, it's okay, that's not cheating. What thoughts or feelings do you have about your answer?

4. Where in your life as a Lightworker do you feel you could use more grounding?

Chapter 2:

Grounding Methods

There are many ways to ground, and while we will cover plenty inside this book, you may also find that you yourself have other ways that you like to ground. You may also notice that certain people or things, like objects of comfort, spaces, geographic locations, personal items, groups of people, songs, foods, books, quotes, movies, etc., have a grounding effect on you. We are fans of "whatever works" so by all means, keep using whatever is working for you as far as grounding goes. The purpose of this book is to expand your knowledge and awareness around grounding, and to help you to consistently create even more grounding for yourself and the people you love.

In this chapter, we'll look specifically at types of methods, and then in the next few chapters, we'll get into the nitty gritty specifics of how to ground using passive, active, and combination methods. Ready? Let's go.

Nature

What do you notice when you go outside and connect with nature? This could be as simple as a leisurely walk, watching a sunset, or gazing at the clouds. Or it could be more interactive, like gardening, photographing trees, hunting for cool rocks, playing in a stream, or walking barefoot in the grass. Just stepping outdoors provides a swift grounding effect for many people. This is a big reason why so many Lightworkers enjoy hosting and attending retreats, as these are usually located in scenic, serene settings and include time spent outdoors.

Amy Scott Grant: I Hugged a Tree... Once.

I'm not what you would call a "nature girl" by any stretch of the imagination. I don't like bugs, I don't like to sweat, and I prefer to wear sparkly flip flops outdoors, even when it's snowing. But in my line of work as a Spiritual Ass Kicker, there's a lot of talk about tree hugging. Eventually, I began to wonder if I was missing out on something amazing.

So, just once, I hugged a tree. It was itchy, and I did not like it.

I could swear the tree was annoyed by my impromptu embrace, like when I was a kid and that one aunt would pinch my cheek in some bizarre and ancient sign of affection. Plus, I worried ants would crawl onto my arms and bite me the whole time. Even now, I shudder when I think of it.

And yet, there is something amazingly grounding and soothing about spending time outdoors. Even for me.

That's because nature is, well, naturally grounding. When you consider that grounding is all about an earth connection, it makes sense that the closer you get to the earth, the stronger the connection, and the easier it is for you to ground.

Some people will tell you that you need to remove your shoes and socks and stand on bare earth (dirt or sand). Surprisingly, not all of these people are rednecks or hippies. We would advise you to check in and do whatever is optimal for you. If you don't know what we mean when we say "check in," then do yourself a favor and grab a copy of *Pendulum Mojo: How to Use Truth Testing for Clarity, Confidence, and Peace of Mind*.

When it comes to grounding, almost any kind of outdoor experience will do the trick. It could be as simple as a casual walk outside; it doesn't have to be a twelve-mile hike into a natural forest, or a three-day camping excursion, or a white-water rafting trip. By the way, if you think it's impossible to ground while navigating raging rapids, take a closer peek at your guide next time. These river guides are so comfortable on the water, you can see how grounded they are inside that raft. Even though many of them look a bit leathery and may be chronic pot smokers (let's face it, in Colorado they probably are), they are swift to move expertly into action when one of their charges has an oopsie, like falling out of the raft into the current. They are cool and collected on the water, because they have learned to be grounded there.

Likewise, very experienced Lightworkers have learned to remain grounded no matter what their clients may be feeling or expressing. Amy once had a client who would scream at her from time to time. And while Amy would certainly not tolerate such behavior in any other setting or situation, she was able to remain grounded during sessions with this particular client. This allowed Amy to simply hold space for the client with the awareness that her screaming had nothing whatsoever to do with Amy herself, and was simply a tool for this client to move through very painful and frustrating emotions. The same is true for seasoned Lightworkers who can remain grounded and hold space for clients who are overcome with difficult emotions, who are relating the details of an especially painful experience, who are caught up in their head, or who are scattered and unable to focus, or who are caught up in the depths of despair. By remaining grounded, we give our clients the safe space they need so that we can help them to heal. And as we mentioned earlier, remaining grounded throughout a healing session helps prevent you from picking up those adverse thoughts, feelings, or energy from each and every person you provide Lightworking services to.

Lisa Dyck: Pennies and Bonfires

Nature is one of the easiest and most proficient ways to ground your multidimensional bodies. As an adult, I consciously learned about grounding and how to do so when I enrolled in my first level Reiki. When I think back to being a child, I realized that I somehow innately knew how to ground. My mother couldn't keep me out of the garden or the flower beds. I was totally that kid that would climb trees and then scream for my dad to bring the ladder to save me, because I had climbed too high and couldn't get back down on my own. I also belonged to the "weird" group of kids at school who would pick the little white stones off the side of the school and turn them into pretty colours by colouring them with markers. And we can't forget the extensive collection of sparkly stones that I collected while walking down the gravel road from our farm to the neighbors and back. I am proud to say that the sparkly stones have now progressed into a beautiful collection of crystals.

Some of the quick fixes I use to ground with nature are to stand barefoot on the grass, lie on the ground watching the clouds go by, gardening, or burying myself up to my waist on a sandy beach. Not all of these options are available during the winter months in Canada, so even bundling up and hugging a tree in the dead of winter works. But my absolute, all-time favourite way to ground in nature is to head out to the nearby river with a penny in my pocket. The Souris River is not very deep during the hot summer months, and you can walk right across the waist-deep water from bank to bank in most spots. Its edges are mostly grey shale with very little sand, but you can always find a large rock to sit on near the water. By lighting a small bonfire close to the rock and tossing a couple of pennies into it, it enables me to incorporate all of the elements of air, fire, water, earth, and metal.

Once the bonfire is lit and the copper pennies have been tossed in, you can see the orange flames laced with green from the hot pennies. Picture yourself perched on a rock with your feet in the water, eyes closed, and a light breeze tickling your face. Tuning into the sounds of the river running by, the birds singing, the wind rustling through the leaves of the trees. The breeze also carries the smell of the water, the shale, and the fire crackling beside you. Visualizing energy entering your crown chakra and setting the intention to release what isn't serving you or whatever is weighing you down, allows the water to carry it all away from your root chakra, cleansing your mind, body, and soul. Incorporating all the elements is the most powerful and effective way for me to ground in nature.

Grounding in nature can involve whatever you like: hiking, sitting in the grass, watching a sunrise or sunset, hugging a tree (watch out for those ants), enjoying your morning beverage on the patio or veranda, opening a window and sitting near it, grilling outdoors, or taking a walk. These are only a few suggestions, and you are limited only by your imagination.

Walking outside is a quick and effective way to ground. Amy has advised many ungrounded clients in the corporate realm to eat their lunch outdoors when possible. If the weather is prohibitive, eat lunch in a solarium or atrium where you can see the outdoors and feel the sunlight on your body. Even a five-minute jaunt outside is enough to ground most people for the next few hours, which is long enough to make it through the rest of the workday in most cases.

Amy Scott Grant: Muttering Like a Crazy Person

Years ago, when I first began to write, my daily routine included an outdoor walk. I quickly discovered the impact of these walks. Specifically, whether or not I walked each day made a substantial difference in whether or not I felt like writing, and how much. Additionally, I noticed the decision to walk or not to walk on any given day had a profound effect on my mood for the rest of the day. My favorite time of year to walk is in the fall, when the air is cool and crisp and the sky is deeply blue. If you start walking for the sake of grounding (as opposed to walking for exercise), you may quickly find that you settle into a rhythm and a timing that works for you. Yes, the purpose of your walk actually matters, although exercise is a nice by-product of walking for grounding.

For example, when I walk for grounding and clarity, I have found that forty to sixty minutes is the ideal time frame for me. For the first ten to twenty minutes, my brain is churning. I'm actively mulching through the day's challenges and to-dos. My head is usually tilted down and I probably look like a crazy homeless person, unaware of her surroundings and muttering to herself incoherently. But after several minutes, something opens up and my head feels much clearer and more settled.

At this point, my pace changes, my posture improves, my head is now upright, and I begin to notice my surroundings. I may hear the crunch of fallen leaves beneath my feet, or notice a particularly interesting tree, or the color of the sky, or some other lady walking around with her head down, muttering to herself... at which point, I try not to pass judgment. My head feels serene and peaceful, and it is a form of meditation for me. Then typically, the last third of my walk is when the ideas begin to flow. Sometimes, solutions present

32

themselves so quickly and with such fervor that I hurry my step or perhaps jog the rest of the way home, eager to get to work and begin implementation of these fresh ideas.

I am truly grateful that I work from home and have extremely flexible hours; plus, I live next to a park and several walking trails. Yet, at the same time, I realize not everyone has this luxury.

This may all seem fine and good if, like Amy and Terry, you live in a beautiful suburban area of Colorado or California. But if you live and work inside the concrete jungle, or you live in an area with harsh weather and forbidding outdoor conditions, you might find yourself wondering how you can ground in nature without easy access to trees and sky and trails.

The answer is simpler than you think. If you can't go outside to be in nature or if it doesn't feel very natural outside where you live, then bring nature inside to you! You can bring the grounding elements of the outdoors into your indoor living space in countless ways. Here are a few suggestions:

- **Art.** Whether you're in a cubicle or a studio apartment, there is surely a wall or flat surface in need of a little artistic expression. Consider art that suggests or features trees, landscapes, mountains, forests, plants, etc. The art may be three-dimensional like a sculpture or shadow box, photography, painting, mosaics, a child's drawing, a collage of nature you make yourself, or anything that feels calming to you.

- **Home décor.** Consider decorating with natural elements such as wood (from picture frames to a farmhouse chic table), leaves (from silk arrangements to dried or pressed leaves or flowers), sand and shells from a beach vacation, or perhaps a basket of pinecones. You can buy these at a craft store or order online if there are no pine trees in your area. Give yourself extra credit if the pinecones are cinnamon or evergreen scented. Even fresh flowers can brighten a room while helping you feel grounded.

- **Plants and trees.** These are perhaps the quickest way to ground a space by bringing nature indoors. For bonus points, place a plant or tree in the prosperity corner of your home or office. What? You haven't taken Amy's feng shui course yet? Stand in the entryway to the space and look to the far-left corner to locate your prosperity gua.

- **Dream board.** You can create a traditional dream board by adhering images to a large flat surface, like a poster board. But you can also create the effect of a dream board by strategically placing suggestive images in your space. For example, to bring nature into your space, you might get some "outdoor life" magazines to stack or spread nearby. Hang a nature-themed calendar in your kitchen or your bathroom. Wait, you still use old-fashioned paper calendars, right? Okay whew, it's not just us.

- **Computer.** If decorating your space is not an option at all, consider how much time you spend in front of your computer. Why not choose a desktop background image and/or a screen saver of nature images?

Personally, we use a lot of these ideas in our own spaces. In Amy's office at home, there's a live potted tree she calls Betty in the prosperity corner, there's paintings and photography depicting various forms of nature, and the desktop image on Amy's computer is a picture taken in the Rocky Mountain National Forest of Colorado. Amy's office décor includes salt lamps and assorted crystals and rocks, and even a tabletop

Zen rock garden. This room has three large picture windows featuring views of the backyard trees, and when the trees are bare in winter, you can see the mountains. A quick glance out the window at any time of day provides her with immediate grounding.

Terry's home features numerous plants and animals. Terry takes excellent care of the animals but thank goodness for Terry's husband, otherwise those plants would have shriveled up long ago! Throughout Terry's home and home office, you'll find earthy touches like granite countertops and warm, earth toned throws, pillows, and upholstery. Most rooms feature the glow of a Himalayan salt lamp alongside crystals, healing tools, and artwork. The entire back side of Terry's home offers picture windows with sweeping California mountain views.

Now you just really want to come visit and see for yourself, right? If you like, you could take a few minutes right now to glance around your own space and jot down some ideas about how you can bring nature inside to help ground and center you. Pay special attention to any space where you conduct healing work or Lightworking—these are spaces that deserve to have kisses of nature providing steady, stable grounding energy for you. More about that in just a bit.

Connecting to the Earth

Some folks call it "earthing" and while you could buy a whole book or visit entire websites devoted to earthing, we will tell you what it is and how to do it in a single paragraph.

Stand or walk barefoot on raw earth. Try it on dirt, grass, rocks (careful!), stones, in streams and riverbeds, in forests, and on hiking trails. Walk barefoot on fallen pine needles, sandy beaches, even in the snow. But watch out for the yellow snow. Seriously, there are tons of highly absorbent receptors on the bottom of your feet, which is why some folks wear flip flops in any public shower, even in hotel showers. Hey, at least yellow snow gives you a visual warning that it's unclean!

Barefoot running is gaining in popularity, as runners enjoy the experience of earthing combined with the runner's high. Amy hasn't personally tried it because a) she hates running and b) she would totally obsess about stepping on spiders, rusty nails, or dog poop. Ewww. Luckily, you don't have to run barefoot to connect to the earth; you can simply cast aside those fancy shoes and socks and stand anywhere outside. Grass and sand feel especially nice, but feel free to go with whatever feels best to you or is readily available.

Sarah A. Sherman: The Mountain

In front of me was a mountain. Not too tall, not too short. A beautiful mountain set in the Sacred Valley. Its side was craggy with rocks and occasional vegetation. The sun shone on its side every afternoon as it set. It created a beautiful play of light upon it. The mountains surrounding the valley are the kind that make you want to stop just to inhale their beauty. Kissed deeply by snow, their peaks rose high into the heavens. You could feel the majestic stillness of this place. The Sacred Valley is not your normal valley. It is a very ancient place. All around it, you can see the stories of the people who lived there before. Ancient paths and footprints. You can see deep roots through time. Megaliths and ruins, some so old that people have lost the way to create the very steps I take on my journey. Some mysteries have grown silent in time. My mind wanted to tangle me standing at the base of this mountain. Stories and reflections wanted to call me away declaring their importance. Exhaling, I became a state of no thought, mindlessness. Some people hold the opinion that this state is where we accomplish the most. Detaching from our fears, projections from people who do not know or understand, distractions....

Climbing this mountain required me to become present with creation and my path. As I looked at the head of the mountain, I knew the effort that it would take to get there. I pulled my straw hat low over my eyes, shading myself from the sun. I tugged my pack over my shoulders feeling the presence of the water I carried with me. Thanking all of creation and the Great Spirit for the shoes that held my feet, I began to climb. One step at a time. I knew I would get there. These steps were ancient, the rocks carved from stone from a quarry found miles away. They are absolutely nothing like the steps we make today, ones that are even and precise. These steps are rugged and wild and varied. Solid. They shone with a smoothness of the footsteps of many. The steps were carved from stone, yet the heights were all uneven. Some steps were just cuts in giant rock outcroppings. Parts of the way, I crawled. On the flat dirt paths, I walked. The way the path was designed, you had to be fully present in the moment. The way to walk was being thoughtless in the now. Feeling, seeing, in experience.

The first hikes, I could sense tension deep in me, a distraction. Like the nights when you wanted to lay down to sleep but conversations from years ago want to replay in your mind. Connecting with my breath and the moment. Early on, the tension created the thoughts. My foot connection with the rocks would fade and I would go a million miles away. Reigning these thoughts back into nothingness became the pattern of my footsteps until I only heard the footsteps, the sun, and the birds singing a song. At the top of the mountain, I rested, my soul lifting prayers of thanksgiving and gratitude for this beautiful day.

Some Lightworkers incorporate a brief grounding at the beginning of each session. This is useful for both the Lightworker and the client, as it serves to ground both individuals as well as the space in which they are working.

Amy Scott Grant: The Grounding Cord

When I'm on the phone with a client who isn't grounded, this is the method I typically walk them through to quickly ground them, so we can get to work and have a more productive session.

> *Stand with your feet planted firmly on the ground, weight distributed evenly between both feet. Relax your knees. Close your eyes and relax. Relax your jaw, your shoulders, and your tongue.*

> *Imagine there is a cord, any kind of cord or rope or string, running from the base of your spine all the way down to the center of the earth. This cord connects you, and you feel safe and grounded because of it. Now imagine that there is a funnel above your head, with the narrow part of the funnel leading down into your crown and the wide part of the funnel reaching up into the sky.*

Congratulations, you're grounded! Now if you like, you can take it a step further and run some energy up and down. Most people find this to be a very pleasant experience:

> *Imagine that you are pulling energy up from the earth's core and allowing this energy to comfortably travel up your body, straight up in a line, and then it moves up and out through your crown. Now imagine that you are reaching high into the sky and pulling energy from the sky down through your funnel and into your crown. This energy travels down your body, down into your feet.*

> *You can run this energy up and down your body as often as you wish, or you could stop here. When you*

feel relaxed, connected, energized, and expanded, it is complete.

Grounding Stones

Certain rocks or gemstones have a very earthy, grounding effect. This is often due to their color or composition. Here are just a few examples of excellent stones for grounding:

- Black or dark stones like obsidian, black tourmaline, hematite*, smoky quartz, onyx, jet, magnetite, and brown sardonyx.
- Earthy-colored stones like red jasper, tiger iron (different from tiger's eye), bloodstone, moss agate, fire agate, and unakite.
- Also stones such as turquoise, galena, tourmalinated quartz, kyanite, any kind of agate, and any kind of jasper.
- Additionally, it's not just crystals and gemstones that are useful for grounding – any earthy stones like boulders, river rocks, etc., or even stoneware and ceramics can be incorporated to create a grounding effect.
- While not technically stones, salt lamps and carvings made from pink Himalayan salt make excellent grounding tools. Salt lamps are widely available, most recently making their way into mainstream stores such as HomeGoods, Bed Bath & Beyond, and the Home Depot.

For an in-depth look at crystals and their uses, check out our absolute fave crystal resource: *The Crystal Bible* series by Judy Hall.

* **NOTE:** You know how Sudafed makes some people sleepy, yet makes other people as hyper as a toddler on Halloween?

Well, hematite works the same way, so it's best to Truth Test this stone to discern whether it will serve as a grounding tool for you personally. If you don't know how to Truth Test, pop over to Amazon and get yourself a copy of *Pendulum Mojo*.

Actually, that's good advice for any stone—make sure it's going to be effective in grounding YOU, no matter what anyone else says (even Judy Hall).

Grounding Mats and Tools

A quick internet search will reveal countless assorted items that claim to be effective grounding tools. There are grounding mats as small as a drink coaster or large enough to cover the space under a king-sized bed and everywhere in-between, special socks and gloves, jewelry, clothing, metal-framed sacred geometry structures designed to wear atop your head, huge pyramids you can sit inside, water bottles designed to ground your water, and all sorts of stuff. "Earthing" tools are one of those things that can really get people's freak flag flying.

We're not saying they don't work, mind you. We happen to own a few of those stainless steel water bottles with the crystals set in resin on the bottom, which claim to purify and charge your water with all kinds of good stuff. Like anything, the deciding factor as to whether or not something works for you is often what you believe about it. We know people who have spent hundreds of dollars on a grounding mat and they swear by it. They claim they can't sleep anywhere else without that grounding mat under their bed. We also know people who own the exact same mat and feel it does nothing for them at all.

There are tons of these products on the market, and whether or not you choose to buy any is entirely up to you. We personally find some of the items to be gimmicky, while others are appealing, and still others make us think, "We could do the same thing with crystals we already own."

But then again, we are both naturally grounded individuals. We don't require as much external grounding support as a naturally ungrounded person. Hell, every book Amy writes has grounding built into it, simply because it was written by her. We can't help but ground every place we go; it's how we're built. Even this very book is a grounding tool. Because of its built-in grounding properties, you might notice this book relaxes you, or makes you feel safe and cozy. If you're naturally grounded, you might not have noticed because you were already grounded. Either way, you're welcome. *wink*

Amy Scott Grant: My $40 Solution

If you've watched my YouTube videos on Truth Testing, you likely saw the one where I explain how to use an etheric weaver. At the end of the video, I explain how you can actually use any pendulum to do the same type of healing as the rather pricey weaver... a point which is not too popular among people who've already sunk a hundred and fifty bucks on an authentic weaver. Perhaps you're wondering if the same is true for grounding mats. Read on to find out.

My office in my home is carpeted, and I love this space. But soon after we moved in, I quickly found the plush carpet in my office to be impractical with the rolling wheels of my ergonomic desk chair. My chair wheels were chewing up the carpet, so I went out in search of a solution. I didn't like any of the plastic carpet protectors you see in offices. They all looked weird and cheap to me, even the very expensive ones! Plus they smelled weird, and they felt way too corporate. This is my home office, after all. There's a super fluffy Turkish rug in the middle of the room, and a sofa bed with a soft plushy throw for lounging about, beautiful lighting, big windows, salt lamps and photos—the room just feels amazing. It would have wrecked the vibe of the whole room if I had thrown some industrial-strength plastic sheet under my desk.

I went a-searching and found no suitable solutions, until suddenly, an idea struck me. I bought a thin indoor-outdoor rug, which was the perfect size for everywhere my chair would roll. It protects my plushy carpet, allows the wheels to roll easily—which a fine rug like my Turkish beauty would simply not permit—and it matches the décor of my office.

Can you guess what color I chose? Yep, I only just realized it while writing this very chapter, but the very rug on top of which my butt resides comfortably in my ergo desk chair, even right now as I type these very words—this rug is brown.

Do you see what I mean about naturally grounding? I wasn't thinking about grounding when I bought this rug. I simply needed a solution to protect my floor, and to ensure my chair would roll easily when I wanted it to. And yet, I wound up purchasing the most grounding color there is, to rest beneath me all the time that I'm Lightworking.

Could I have used a $250 grounding mat instead? I'm sure I could have. But this rug does the trick, looks nicer, and cost a whole lot less… about forty bucks, if you must know.

If you are not naturally grounded, you will likely require more of the solutions in this book than someone who is naturally grounded. But please do not feel you need to go crazy buying up all the grounding tools you can find. Some are quite expensive, so we highly recommend Truth Testing before you buy any grounding tools online. In many cases, there are other less expensive substitutes like a rug or a big fluffy brown blanket that work just as well and won't clash with the décor of your space. In the how-to chapters that follow, we'll even show you how to create your own grounding tools.

But it's nice to know these grounding tools exist on the market, isn't it? Personally, we like having options; it makes us feel powerful and discerning. Like right now, when we get to choose which topic we'll cover next. Ah, here we go:

Activating the Root Chakra

Do you know about your chakra system? If not, here's a lightning fast explanation of this amazing energy system you can harness to make your life better in countless ways (for now, we're just going to focus on grounding).

There are channels of energy that run inside your body at the energetic level, also called the subtle body. Many chakras exist, but when you hear people talk about the "chakra system," they're usually referring to the seven main chakras as pictured below, bottom to top: root, sacral, solar plexus, heart, throat, third eye, and crown.

Despite the way our lovely model is sitting in the image, the root chakra is not at your ankles – it's actually located at the base of your spine at the tailbone (coccyx). C'mon, say it out loud with us, it's fun. "Coccyx." If you say it three times fast, it starts to sound dirty. Just kidding. This chakra is dead serious: it's your foundation of support and stability. A well-balanced root chakra means you are grounded, centered, and secure. This explains why nearly all chakra healing work begins with the root chakra. Remember Maslow's Hierarchy of needs? Safety and security is the bottom of the pyramid—without it, there's no solid foundation upon which to build.

The root chakra is all about getting your basic survival needs met: food, shelter, clothing, and enough money to cover your bills. When this chakra is unbalanced, illness can occur, or worse. Balancing this chakra brings safety and a sense of security. The color most often associated with the root chakra is a dark or ruddy red.

Amy Scott Grant: Yep, I Admit It

At the risk of sounding like a total dork, I confess that I love, love, love my root chakra. Before I dove into my intuitive gifts, my root was extremely blocked. Today it grounds me 24/7, effortlessly. It works so hard for me and for everyone I heal, and it is a huge reason that I am able to cause miracles for people. The energy in the room shifts when I walk into it, and as much as I'd like to believe it's charm or charisma or perhaps fabulous style and good looks, it's really as simple as this:

I hold a massive grounding energy all around me, and when people meet me, they feel it. Thank you, root chakra. You rock.

If you have any experience with energy work or energy healing, you already know how important it is to keep the chakras open and balanced, otherwise illness or other issues can occur.

Balancing the chakras is a relatively simple process, but it's not permanent. Think of it as hydration. You'll never be "finished" drinking water because the body needs constant hydration in order to perform its essential processes. Drink as much water as you want now, and you will still grow thirsty again later, and eventually need more water. The same is true when you balance your chakras. Balanced, open chakras feel wonderful, but through the course of living life day to day, you will soon need to rebalance your chakras again.

All of the grounding methods in this book will help to open and balance your root chakra, but there are some specific ways to tap into root chakra energy and get it grounding for you. We'll cover these in detail in the "how to" chapters.

Settling in

Perhaps one of the most intuitive or natural ways to ground is what we simply call "settling in." You do it any time you meditate or listen to a guided mediation or visualization. You also do this if you take yoga, tai chi, martial arts, or any other type of mindfulness class. Settling in is when you settle into your body, relax, and get comfortable. Children do this when nestling down into their bed before sleepy time. Children participating in Romper Room are demonstrating the exact opposite of settling in. Settling in is a quick and easy way to ground before beginning a session for Lightworking, and you may find you already do this quite naturally at these times.

Breath Work

Again, if you take yoga, tai chi, martial arts, Lamaze, or any other kind of training that focuses on mind-body connection, then you are most likely already doing some breath work. In the how-to sections that follow, we will specifically explore breathing exercises that create a grounding effect.

Body Work

Body work is extremely popular among seekers and Light-workers. This includes hands-on physical touch, such as therapeutic massage, intuitive massage, cranio-sacral massage, lymphatic drainage, chiropractic work, acupressure and acupuncture, EFT Emotional Freedom Technique, etc. This would also include body work done at the subtle energy level, such as Reiki. When receiving treatment in the form of body work, you can often tell how focused and grounded your practitioner is by noticing how quickly he or she is able to ground you. Beware the body work practitioner who arrives for your appointment frazzled, tardy, or out of sorts!

Courtney Harper: Grounding Through Physical Touch

The sweetest, most satisfying grounding method I like to employ is physical touch. When I'm disconnected from my body, feeling the skin of another person (or animal!) can bring me back to Mama Earth quicker than anything else. If I can hold or be held, all the more effective. I discovered the value in grounding energy through physical touch by interacting with my daughters. I noticed that they would calm down when I held them for a while (no surprise there), but when I held them before or after a change or a bath, I noticed they relaxed significantly faster. Once I realized this happened because we were mostly skin-to-skin during these transitions, everything changed! Now if my girls are inconsolable, I rub their backs, hold their hands, or stroke their arms and the grounding happens nearly instantly. Added bonus: I just grounded my energy too! So now, rather than getting caught up in the overwhelm myself, I can see through that tantrum and get to the issue behind the tissue.

Grounding through physical touch benefits my husband as well, for reasons you might intuit because... well, you're psychic, am I right?? But also because physical touch between romantic partners is most intense during sex. If you experience an orgasm, the grounding effects go even deeper as our physical bodies don't experience very many sensations more pleasurable than that. So what if you don't have a partner or a child handy and you REALLY need some grounding? I recommend a good, old-fashioned embrace! Just a simple hug can connect you to another person. When we're connected to each other, we're connected to Gaia. And when we're connected to Gaia, we are—by definition—grounded. Grounding by physical touch: quick, easy, and collaborative!

In the next chapter, we'll explore passive ways to ground. But first, please take a few minutes to write down your answers to these Food for Thought questions.

Chapter 2 Food for Thought: yummy

1. When do you feel most connected to nature?

2. Where in nature do you feel the most grounded? How often do you make time for this? How do you feel about your answer?

3. What rooms or areas in your home could benefit from bringing in some elements of the outdoors for the purpose of grounding? What about in your work space? In spaces where you perform Lightworking? In other areas?

4. Do you currently own grounding tools or items that you're not currently using? If so, how could you incorporate these into the areas you listed in question #3?

Chapter 3:
Passive Ways to Ground

Now that we're diving into specific methods for grounding, let's first look at passive ways to ground because hey, these are easy! A great deal of your success with passive grounding methods will depend upon your intention. Intention is defined as "an aim or plan," and it is as simple as deciding what you want the outcome to be and clarifying that intention with a verbal or written statement or a simple thought or mental image. For example, your intention might be stated as "I intend to feel safe and calm and grounded whenever I wear this necklace." Easy, right?

Farah McCallum: Hot White Chocolate Mocha

I was raised in a very Christian home. I was born when my father was in Bible college in Colorado Springs in the mid-'70s. There was not a lot of room in my life for "grounding" or anything other than a prayer to Jesus. I have to say though, as Christian as my family is, they have always supported me in my crazy unpredictable life. One day back in 2006, I got itchy feet and I knew it was time to pack up and move on with my life (that's another story for another time), but I knew I had to get movin' along and I got this crazy hair up my back side that said, "Move to Istanbul, Turkey and teach English." Wait, what? Yup, that is what my hair was telling me! This is where my first grounding experience came in. Now, I was no spring chicken, but I was not about to argue with the "hair." Nope! So I set out to move my cute self to Turkey. I was not scared to move. Not at all. But I was terrified to fly. I had flown many times in the past but not since 9/11. Ohhh! What was I going to do? I was all OVER the place energetically about flying and I was going halfway around the freaking world. OMG. And then out of the blue (or not) came Cindy.

Cindy was a friend of my BFF Christina Hayes (awesome lightworker). I did not really know Cindy but she was my light at the moment I needed it. My plans were coming along to quit my job and go on this crazy adventure when I ran into Cindy at Starbucks. What are the odds, right? That she would be at the Starbucks next to my work at precisely my break time. Divine timing perhaps? After the, "oh hey, how are you?" awkward moment when you don't really know someone but recognize them and must be polite, she quietly asked me how I was. I said, "great" and proceeded to tell her I was moving and was just a little freaked out to fly. She said nothing but put her hand about 3 inches above my head, waved it around like she was giving me a halo (which I do deserve, by the way!) And at that moment, standing in line at Starbucks waiting to get my hot white chocolate mocha, I felt the ground swell up around me and bring all my energy, which I'm sure had reached the moon by now, come back home to rest peacefully inside me. Amazing! I have never once, from that moment on, had one smidgen of anxiety about flying, to this day! She grounded me and now when I need to ground myself I just imagine the halo above me and imagine the ground below me and I am all set to conquer the world.

The use of passive grounding methods helps you to ground 24/7 without additional or ongoing effort. These are set-it-and-forget-it forms of grounding you can start using now to feel more grounded immediately. If you are not a naturally grounded person, you're going to want to incorporate passive, active, and maybe some combination methods, so we might as well dive in to the easiest ones of the lot. And finally, if you are a naturally grounded person, you're probably ready to cut to the chase anyway, so let's jump in and get grounded!

Nature

Nature is one of the most passive ways to ground, as it merely requires you to be out in it. Sit on the deck and sip your morning coffee, take a stroll around the park, or gaze out of the window. Boom, you're grounded. *mic drop*

Terry Robnett: Lying Down in the Park

Have you ever just laid on your back in the park, your front lawn, or even in the backyard, and just stared at the sky? Isn't it miraculous? There is something so inexplicably incredible about that simple action of really doing nothing but being.

*WOW! Did you just get an a-ha moment? Because I seriously just did while writing this. The a-ha moment is that doing nothing and just **being** is what meditation is all about. Meditation is actually a form of grounding. Did you know that? If not, you know now.*

Lying in the park is definitely a natural form of grounding that awards you the opportunity to be one with nature by just being. It literally requires nothing from you but to just relax your mind and body, maybe close your eyes for a bit so that you can refuel. Heck, you can even get in a nap! How awesome is that? Sometimes I will even lay with my feet against the trunk of a tree to share space. Maybe even

51

exchange energy. *This is such a simple but beneficial mindless task that anyone can do to successfully ground.*

Stones and Crystals

You can refer back to the list of grounding stones in the prior chapter, but after you purchase some grounding crystals, here are a number of ways you can use them, whether you're actively Lightworking or not:

Carry a small grounding stone in your pocket. If you're wearing jeans, the quarter pocket/condom pocket is a great place to stash a small grounding stone. A pocket is more effective than a purse, since it's closer to your body, and for longer periods of time. A small, flat stone works well for this. Caveat: be sure to remove the stone before undressing, as some stones will not survive a fall to the floor, much less a full cycle through the washer and dryer.

Wear jewelry that contains grounding stones. You can purchase such jewelry or make your own. Certain stones are most helpful when placed over certain parts of the body. Again, if you're interested in learning more about crystals and their uses, you should really treat yourself to a copy of *The Crystal Bible* by Judy Hall.

If you have trouble sleeping, or experience restless sleep, ***place a grounding stone under your bed,*** either where your head normally rests, under your butt with the intention that it's opening and activating your root chakra, or under your feet, or all three.

Create a grid with grounding stones. There are many different ways to do this, and some folks will disagree with what we're about to tell you, but in our experience, you don't need any special training to know how to set up a crystal grid. Gasp! Did we just say that out loud? Simply follow your intuition and let the stones themselves guide your placement. Most importantly, place these stones with intention, such as: to ground you, your space, everyone who uses or frequents the space, a particular project, etc. You can leave the grid in place as long as feels optimal, and it will continue working for you tirelessly.

If a house, building, structure, or property needs grounding, you can **bury stones in strategic spots to help ground the entire space.** This form of intentional placement may or may not represent a type of grid. For example, you might bury a stone at the four corners of the property to create a grid and ground the entire property. Or you might just choose to bury a stone in or surrounding a spot that feels particularly ungrounded. For example, a steep slope, a sunken hole, under a second-story deck, or the place where they found ol' Red had up and died. Rest in peace, Red.

Place stones in areas where you spend a lot of time, where you perform Lightworking, or wherever you are likely to become ungrounded. For example, if driving stresses you out, then we would definitely recommend putting some grounding stones in your car and letting them do the heavy lifting for you. You can place them on the floor underneath the driver's seat—which puts 'em right under your root chakra—in the console, or in the glove box. Incidentally, what do people call that today? The forward compartment? Dashboard? Does anyone actually keep gloves in that box anymore? Amy's is full of car paperwork, tampons, ketchup packets, and a couple of emergency snacks for the kids. No gloves, though. Which would be unfortunate if she ever decides to challenge someone to a duel.

Meditate with stones. This is as easy as it sounds. Simply meditate as you normally would, but before you do, place stones *with intention*. This might entail placing stones on or around yourself, or elsewhere in your immediate environment.

For added grounding, you can sit on a stone (a small, flat one... otherwise, it could seriously get uncomfortable, depending on what you're into). Some people put stones in their underwear or bra to keep the stones close to their body. The only caveat with this is you may eventually forget they're there and suddenly find yourself flushing with embarrassment when you stand up or lean over and a stone falls out of your bosom or pants! It's downright hilarious when it happens to someone else, though.

If you find a shape that feels just right in your hand, you can **use a grounding stone as a "worry stone."** A worry stone, also called a "thumb stone," is a small, smooth, rather flat polished stone, sometimes with a thumb-sized indentation on one surface. Hold the stone in one hand in such a way as to be able to gently rub your thumb forward and back through the indentation, a process that is often soothing. No one knows for certain which culture first invented the worry stone, which dates back to ancient folk practices in Greece, Tibet, Ireland, and several Native American tribes, but worry stones are still widely used today. And just because you use a worry stone, it doesn't mean you'll start worrying more, in case you were worried about that. As our friends down under say, "No worries, mate!" Except if you ever heard a real Aussie say it, it winds up sounding more like "nohwarresmayt." Damn, now Amy suddenly has a hankering for TimTams, Cherry Ripes, and Violet Crumble. Can we skip ahead to the Food for Thought section? Oops! Got ungrounded there for a second. And... we're back.

You can also **use a grounding stone to make an elixir.** This involves placing the stone in water for a few days or longer, intending that the properties of the stone are transferred to the water. The water can then be used in a variety of ways: added to drinking water, sprinkled over a bath, shpritzed on the skin, etc. If you've ever seen the movie *What the Bleep Do We Know?* or you've learned anything about Dr. Emoto's work,

54

then this concept probably makes sense to you. Otherwise, you might suspect our cheese has slid clean off our cracker. But crystal elixirs are definitely "a thing" and you can learn more about them in Judy Hall's *The Crystal Bible*. Of note, why is "shpritzed" not in the spell check dictionary? Shouldn't every Yiddish word become an official part of the English language?

There are other, more obscure uses for crystals and grounding. For example, "the bottle with the nice butt" from VibesUp.com has crystals embedded into resin, which is then permanently adhered to the bottom of a stainless steel water bottle. This bottle is purported to enhance your drinking water by infusing that crystal energy into whatever is inside the bottle. Did you say vodka? Hey, we're not judging, just wanted to make sure we heard you right. We all have our vices. And speaking of intoxication, did you know the ancient Greeks believed that if you drank wine from an amethyst goblet, it would prevent drunkenness? Can't say either of us has ever tested that theory.

With so many ways to use crystals for grounding, why not try out some of the above methods and see which ones work best for you?

Talar Malkhassian: Crystal Improvement

In my few years of life experience (28, to be exact), there are two things I cannot stress enough: self-understanding and self-acceptance. Past that point, everything else just happens naturally.

I've always known I was meant to help others and because of that, I always tried to demand leadership instead of earning it! Then something incredible and life altering happened that saved me. I was hit by a car on November 19, 2008. That accident slowly got me to the mental state I am in today.

55

I currently help others to slowly but surely improve their lives through the healing and elevating powers of well-chosen crystals. What these crystals allow them to do is elevate their mentalities to achieve the goal that they desire. For example: to be less stressed in life, to lose weight, to have more friends, or to attract the love of your life. I have always preferred playing by myself and being alone to being with people, and I finally understood why! I have always felt like I was meant for big things. Amy was the one who told me that the reason I had such a hard time interacting with others was because it was a lesson my soul had given itself to learn in this lifetime. From that moment, my entire perspective on it changed.

After years of slowly but surely working on understanding what I was doing wrong, I came to understand that the problem came when I demanded recognition from others without actually having a reason why I was demanding it! After my accident, all of that changed. Because I had suffered such a big head trauma (the equivalent of a bruise on your brain), I had to relearn how to do everything all over again. Everything from swallowing, standing and sitting straight, walking and talking, all the way to interacting with other people in an amicable way. I also became more attuned to the subtle energies within myself. That is the main reason why I decided to venture down this path in this lifetime.

I always hear about how people have difficulty with understanding and accepting their unique gifts before coming to grips with the fact that they are lightworkers. At this very moment (because I just noticed it myself), I can see that the struggles I had in my life were caused by myself alone! In retrospect, I'm now very comfortable in saying that they were all self-imposed, which tells me that it is what I absolutely needed as a soul in order to graduate to the next level of consciousness. Because of all this hard work I did on myself, I'm very happy to say that I am happier and better placed to help others. I can do this because I put in the work first, unlike when I was a child.

Grounding Mats and Other Tools

Grounding mats and other tools are easy to use. Simply follow the instructions that accompany the tool, and let it do the work for you. Easy peasy lemon squeezy.

For grounding mats, place them on or underneath you, either in direct contact with your body or clothing, or underneath where you sit or lie down, then go about your business. Some very sensitive people find direct contact to be too intense, in which case it's best to have some space or a barrier between you and the mat. Keep this in mind if you're Lightworking face to face with individuals or groups.

Grounding a Space

You can use most any of these passive grounding methods and tools to ground a space by intentionally placing the items in the space, but there is one particular situation worth mentioning. If you live or work above the ground floor, like in an apartment or a high-rise building, we definitely recommend that you place some grounding intention and tools in your space. The same is true if you spend any substantial time in a "hanging" area, like a second-story deck, balcony, or room over a garage or carport. This can be as simple as creating a grid or completing a grid by placing a small grounding stone in each "hanging" corner with the intention that you are grounding that entire room or space.

Most people notice an immediate shift in the way these spaces feel once they are effectively grounded. As a Lightworker, it's always wise to ground a space before and after group work for retreats, workshops, group sessions, couples' sessions, etc.

Massage

When you find a good massage therapist, never let them go! A talented massage therapist can do more than melt away your stress and worries. This person can somehow manage to make you feel safe and cared for, even as you lie naked covered by nothing more than a thin sheet. Simply relaxing and fully enjoying a massage can be extremely grounding. Come to think of it, so can a good pedicure. Yep, we're about due for both of those now... excuse us while we make a couple of quick phone calls.

Color Therapy

Color is an exceptionally passive way to ground. For best results, embrace earthy colors like chocolate brown and brick red. Wear them; choose stones and jewelry in these colors, not to mention a warm and cozy blanket for your bed or your favorite chair. Which reminds us of a story:

Two generals were preparing their soldiers for battle. One general demanded, "Fetch me my red coat."

"But sir," they protested, "if you wear red, the enemy will spot you right away."

"Yes," said the general. "And when I am shot, you will not be able to see the blood dripping down my chest, and so you shall continue to fight without stopping to tend to me."

Hearing this, the second general thought for a moment, and then demanded, "Fetch me my brown pants!"

Jewelry

Earlier, we touched on the idea of wearing jewelry that contains grounding stones and crystals, and what's easier than accessorizing? Well, once you find the proper accessories, of course. But gemstone jewelry isn't the only form of wearable grounding.

Symbols, such as the pyramid, square, triangle, circle, and spiral can all have a grounding effect. Nearly every time you see Amy, she's wearing hoop earrings. She recently learned that the circle not only symbolizes many things, but can also activate healing. Considering she's a full-time healer by occupation, it's no wonder she naturally gravitates toward circles and spirals in her own accessories.

Ladies, the next time your man balks at how much you spend on jewelry, just smile and tell him matter-of-factly that it's necessary for you to be grounded. It's like that great philosopher once said, "Adorn thyself!"

Chocolate!

Yes, chocolate is a grounding food. Think about it, it's warm and brown and makes you feel all cozy inside. What could be more grounding, right? When you eat chocolate, it sends signals to your brain to release endorphins and stimulate other feel-good neurotransmitters. Plus the cacao beans are *ground* to make chocolate. Get it? Because God is not without a sense of humor, and neither are we.

Heck, even fictional characters know about the grounding effects of chocolate. Why do you think Professor Lupin gave chocolate to Harry after he encountered the Dementors in *Prisoner of Azkaban*?

You could argue that chocolate is an active grounding method since you physically have to eat or drink it, but we've included it here among the passive grounding methods because, let's face it—you're probably going to eat it anyway.

Amy Scott Grant: Writing + Chocolate = Happy Ending

When I write, I always have some good quality dark chocolate handy because when I'm writing, I'm more or less channeling, so the chocolate ensures I stay grounded during the process. Sometimes I eat chocolate when I'm not writing, just in case I decide to start writing. Better safe than sorry, right?

Other Grounding Foods

It may surprise you to know that **coffee** is a grounding food, for many of the same reasons as chocolate. Some will find this surprising, since coffee is a stimulant, and too much coffee can definitely cause one to become ungrounded or out of control! We both actually prefer tea over coffee, but we do see the benefits of it, and Amy enjoys cooking with it and eating coffee-infused desserts, like coffee ice cream and tiramisu.

The expression "salt of the earth" will help you remember that **salt** can be a very grounding tool.

Amy Scott Grant: Salt Snob?

Personally, I'm a bit of a salt snob. At any given time, I have upwards of ten different kinds of salt at my house, not one of which is table salt. Yuck! If you've only ever eaten table salt, do yourself a favor and arrange a little taste test where you taste just a bit of: fine Kosher (chef) salt, sea salt, and table salt. Taste the table salt last and you'll quickly notice how harsh and biting it tastes in comparison to a finer quality salt. Celtic grey salt is among my favorites, as is Maldon, a patented finishing salt formed in the shape of pyramid crystals, which makes it doubly grounding. We also keep alder smoked salt on hand, as well as pink Himalayan, Hawaiian black salt, and I could go on and on. What can I say, I love me some salt!

Notice again how the naturally grounded person gravitates toward all things grounding?

Dark leafy greens also have a grounding effect, thanks to their deep, bitter taste and earthy growing conditions. Add these to smoothies, salads, or sauté in oil with a little chopped onion and bacon. Unless you're vegan, then please pass us your bacon, thanks. We'd hate for it to go to waste.

Other grounding sustenance includes foods that grow close to the earth, like beans, legumes, root vegetables such as beets, turnips, parsnips, potato, and sweet potato; and cabbage, squash, and berries. Almonds and tree nuts are also excellent grounding foods, provided you're not allergic (duh).

Hopefully, you're already incorporating these wholesome foods into your daily intake, but if not, you can add them here and there to create more grounding for yourself. It's effective, tasty, and nutritious.

You might be wondering if you actually have to consume the food in order to extract its grounding properties. Nope. Salt lamps are effective at grounding regardless of whether or not you occasionally lick 'em. Sure, you laugh now, but then when we're not looking…. And if you can't stomach kale or root veggies, give 'em a nice fondling the next time you're in the grocery. Oh, please. We've seen how you look at the cucumbers.

Barefootin'

Another passive way to ground is to walk around barefoot. Not across a bed of burning coals, mind you… although Amy has actually done that and it's freaking awesome. You'll want to be quite grounded before considering that, but walking around inside or outside without shoes or socks is very freeing and can quickly connect you to earth energy.

Remember that Turkish rug we mentioned earlier, the one that's in Amy's office? Oh, it is so fabulously soft and sensual on the feet! If Amy gets mentally stuck on something while working, she just walks over to the Turkish rug and shuffles her feet over it, or has a lie down on it, and she instantly feels better. If you've ever seen Russell Brand in the movie *Get Him to the Greek*, then you certainly remember the "stroke the furry wall" scene. Yes, it's exactly like that. Only it's the floor instead of the wall. And no Geoffreys are involved.

Prefer to wear slippers inside? Get yourself a pair of brown house shoes and ground in comfort.

Chapter 3 Food for Thought: deeeeee-lish!

1. Which of the passive grounding methods in this chapter seem most appealing to you?

2. Take a minute to think, then list all the passive grounding methods you're already using. Recognizing them now can help increase their power for keeping you grounded.

3. Referring back to the spaces you listed in Chapter 2 Food for Thought, how can you add in some passive grounding methods and tools to make these spaces feel more grounded?

4. Which passive grounding method in this chapter feels most uncomfortable to you? Are you willing to give it a shot anyway today to test it out? The results just might surprise you!

Chapter 4:

Active Ways to Ground

How to Use a Grounding Cord

It's fairly easy to use a grounding cord, and the good news is you can do it almost anywhere. We don't recommend trying this while driving or operating heavy machinery like a backhoe or vacuum, but it is simple enough to do any time you can be still and close your eyes for just a minute. The grounding cord can be done while sitting, lying, or standing. Here's what you do:

Stand with your feet planted firmly on the ground, weight distributed evenly between both feet. Relax your knees. Close your eyes and relax. Relax your jaw, your shoulders, and your tongue. Imagine there is a cord, any kind of string or rope you like, running from the base of your spine all the way down to the center of the earth. This cord connects you, and you feel safe and grounded because of it. By the way, if this sounds familiar, it's because we already covered it in Chapter 2. But it's arguably the most popular method of grounding, so that makes it worth repeating. In fact, it's not a bad idea to repeat this exercise before starting any kind of Lightworking session.

Etheric Weaver or Pendulum

Amy love love loves her etheric weaver, and she uses it often on friends, family, clients, and herself. In fact, it is one of her most frequently used tools in her Lightworking practice. In case you aren't familiar with this unique healing tool: picture a super fancy pendulum that consists of a large crystal with magnets on either side, all wrapped in wire. Like a quality bra, it's pricey but worth it. To ground with an etheric weaver or with a pendulum, simply do the following:

- relax
- some people find it helps to close your eyes
- hold the weaver or pendulum in a comfortable position and let it swing
- hold the intention that you'll become grounded
- when it stops swinging, boom—you're grounded

Creatively Grounding

For some, the act of creating art can be a very grounding experience. Even though creativity is most closely associated with the sacral chakra, art can center and ground you in a way that is both fun and productive. This might include drawing, coloring (did you know both of your lovely authors have coloring books available on Amazon?), creating mandalas, painting, making jewelry, which is especially effective if you're making grounding jewelry, etc. Creative endeavors keep us balanced and give our inner child an outlet to express herself. "Hey, hey, hey, hey," said Madonna. Because without that creative channel, she gets crabby and starts acting out.

Amy Scott Grant: Like I Need Another Reason to Shop

Sometimes, I find shopping to be a grounding experience, which may or may not be the case for you. For me, it all depends on where I go, what I'm looking for, and how many other people are there. For example, any kind of shopping between Thanksgiving and New Year's is definitely not a grounding experience for me. Likewise, a craft store is typically too stimulating for me, and I usually have to ground just to make it out of there with my sanity intact (what's left of it). The same is true if I'm short on time and have a specific list of items to collect. But if on a random weekday I'm aimlessly wandering around Nordstrom's, or a thrift store, or a craft fair that's not too crowded, the experience unlocks my mind and centers me, giving rise to new ideas and creative solutions. And if I walk away with a few new purchases to boot, that's a total win-win.

Earth Energy

This grounding method requires you to use your imagination. Visualize something that is strongly associated with earth energy. This might include dirt, camping, earthworms, fertile soil, sunflowers, mushrooms, the beach, a forest, potatoes, the smell of your Aunt Peggy, or anything earthy. Hold the vision in your mind's eye until you feel grounded. It's simple, yet effective. This method works especially well when your immediate surroundings do not support grounding. For example, inside a high-rise office, walking the streets of a busy metropolis like New York City (you can just say "New York"), or perhaps while resting for a bit in a straight jacket. What?! We don't know what you do in your spare time.

Susan Church: How to Calm the Storms in Your Life

The first time I heard someone talk about grounding energy as an everyday practice, I saw an image of myself outside during a thunderstorm, with lightning passing through my head, down my body, and harmlessly into the ground. I didn't realize I wasn't that far off. I haven't literally been hit by lightning, but I've learned that taking a few minutes every day to ground myself makes it easier to get through the day without burning out. Sometimes I visualize myself like a tree with roots and branches, especially if I ground myself outside, but most of the time I keep it simple.

1. Stop. Think about it. If you're walking, one foot is always in front of the other. When you stop walking, both feet are on the ground together at the same time. Stand still or sit, as you wish.

2. Breathe. Of course, you breathe all the time without thinking about it, but that's the point. You're bringing your attention to something that is usually automatic. Consciously breathe in and out, deeply, at least twice.

3. Collect your energy. Energy that's scattered all over the place can't be grounded. Call all your energy back to yourself, from wherever it's been.

4. Direct your energy. Draw your energy inside your body, behind your eyes and in front of your spine. Draw it all the way down, into your legs, feet, and toes.

5. Set a grounding cord. Now you're ready to set a grounding cord, which is a connection from the end of your tailbone deep into the earth. The grounding cord can be made of anything you want, such as a tree root, a golden chain, or a giant crystal. It doesn't matter. Whatever will give you a strong connection to the earth. It might even change from one day to the next.

6. Connect. Finally, you're ready for the fun part. You can set your intention for the day, tune into your inner guidance system, or whatever you want. You can run energy from the center below to the center above and back down again. Enjoy!

If you're like me, things will happen during the day to throw you off center. Someone will cut in front of you in traffic or ask you to work on a report at the last minute. You'll think, "What happened? I thought I was cool, calm, and collected. Where's my grounding cord?" Be kind to yourself. Take a few minutes to Stop, Breathe, Collect, Direct, and Set to get grounded and you'll be back on track.

Root Chakra Work

Your root chakra is located at the base of your spine, and there are heaps of ways to activate it:

- Yoga
- Tai Chi
- Pilates
- Martial Arts
- Chanting
- Grunting (primal, guttural)
- Squats
- Marching in place
- High stepping
- Stomping
- Lunges
- Kegels
- Twerking, maybe
- Physical activities that increase your bodily awareness

Let's address some of these in-depth and categorically.

Primal Exercise: We call these activities "primal" because, well, you'll understand when you try them out. Grunting may seem silly, but it transports you back to your caveman days (past life regression, anyone?). Before the invention of our now civilized language—and long before its current degradation— cave people allegedly communicated through a system of grunts and guttural noises. And considering their primary objective was ah ah ah ah stayin' alive, it makes sense that they would have been in touch with their root chakras. Which, in cave speak, was called "Err-uh-ah," or so we've heard.

In present day society, grunting is considered rude, if not offensive. Don't believe it? The next time your boss gives you a task to complete, instead of speaking, just grunt at her and watch what happens. Okay, maybe don't do that in real life. We don't want you to be out of a job and broke because, let's be honest, we have a bunch of cool programs and stuff you're going to want to buy.

Wondering how you can grunt to ground yourself? We're so glad you asked. Right now, exactly where you're sitting, practice grunting. Notice there are two different ways to grunt. One way is to keep your mouth closed and keep the soft to moderate sound in your head—that's not useful for grounding, so don't do that now. The other way is to open your mouth and using your breath, push down or pull up on your diaphragm—the membrane that separates your chest from your abdomen, not the little contraceptive that looks like a trampoline for sperm. Just in case that was unclear. When you grunt in this way, your abdomen should visibly move as you force out the sounds. If you're doing it correctly in public, people would definitely be staring right now. Just wave your club at them threateningly, then scratch your beard and adjust your loincloth and they'll leave you alone.

When you first begin to grunt, you may feel timid, and that sound comes out like a sharp breath. But if you put some oomph into it, you'll soon find you can grunt. Try it now. See what we mean by primal? Feel free to experiment with this for a bit. Notice that you can push harder to get a long, guttural, apelike sound to come out, or you can make the efforts short and abrupt for a more clipped effect. If you're feeling especially cheeky, you might wish to grunt out a particular tune, like the ABC song or Beethoven's Fifth. To ground and activate that root chakra even further, you can grunt while performing squats or lunges, or perhaps twerking?

Physical Exercise: Any kind of activity that moves the body while requiring you to be consciously aware of the body can have a grounding effect. This would also include activities like line dancing, CrossFit®, krav maga, really good sex, and yes, even twerking.

Hold on, we know what you're thinking. Can you really get grounded just by working out and moving? You can if you're focused on your body while you're doing it. For example, banging out 30 burpees while remembering to breathe and not die is a good way to ground. Reading the latest Danielle Steele novel while casually walking on the treadmill is not a good way to ground. Can you see why? The level of intensity is not the giveaway, it's the degree of focus. The first scenario has you focused entirely on your body and the task at hand. You are fully present while doing those diabolical burpees, even though you may be wishing you were anywhere else at that moment. In the second example, you're not at all present or even aware of your body. You're distracting yourself from exercise by reading a novel as a form of escape. More than once we've seen a person fall off a treadmill because they were reading or texting, scarcely aware of their own body. It is the conscious awareness of exercise that creates a grounding effect.

Give yourself bonus points for any physical activity that puts you in touch with your lower half or requires you to really work the area around the root chakra. Specifically, *lunges and squats,* which require you to focus on lowering your root chakra toward the floor, then raising it back up, all while keeping your back and hips in alignment; *kegels,* where you consciously lift and release the pelvic floor; and *high stepping* and *marching in place,* where the majority of movement is focused on the lower half of the body.

Terry Robnett: Grounding with Exercise

Exercise has always been an important part of my life. So, as my journey as a Lightworker evolved, I discovered that there are many forms of exercise that are grounding. Yoga is one of them. And I have watched it, as it becomes more and more popular every day. Yoga is definitely not what it used to be though. It has gotten so much more diverse, a whole lot better with so many more options for everyone from newbies to the most masterful. One can't help but notice both men and women of all ages are engaging in and benefitting from the positive effects of yoga.

I personally never liked yoga until about 15 years ago. What's even funny is for me to state that I never liked yoga was pretty judgmental, since I had never even tried it. I eventually started doing yoga instead of weight lifting due to spinal problems that caught up to me from a neck injury in my teen years. I found that practicing yoga regularly allowed me to remain agile, toned, and fit, which is what I really wanted in the first place. I had no desire to have massive muscles, so this was the perfect exercise for me. The more I did yoga, the more I loved it, and the more I realized how in line it was with where I'm headed in my spiritual life.

For me personally, practicing yoga has served many purposes from getting in physical shape to practicing mindfulness. If you have yet to experience yoga, I more than highly recommend it.

Especially if you are a beginner Lightworker.

You can search YouTube for instructions on the proper execution of all of these activities. Yep, even twerking. But before you do that, keep this in mind: Google owns YouTube, so if you search for something on YouTube, expect that every time you get online for the next three months, your screen will be filled with ads for that very same topic. Heck, we're still seeing ads for caveman costumes since researching information for the previous paragraph.

Stomping is another way to activate the root chakra. Plus, there's a double benefit as your inner child comes out to play. You can combine stomping with grunting for added grounding and root activation. You'll look like a nut, absolutely, but a grounded nut at that. A peanut, perhaps.

Physical Mindfulness: This category typically requires some training to get started, and for proper execution. Yoga, Pilates, and Tai Chi are all excellent forms of physical mindfulness, and we've taken classes for all three of these. Tai Chi is especially grounding, although for us, it's just too slow. No shocker there! But that's the beauty of being alive today—you have more choices than you can shake a stick at. If you don't like one of these methods, try another.

Any of these physical methods for grounding (primal, physical exercise, and physical mindfulness) would be a great addition to in-person Lightworking or group work, as you have the added benefit of being able to demonstrate for your visual learners. Plus, you'll all get to look or sound silly doing it together as a group, which is always more fun than going it alone.

Amy Scott Grant: Surviving Pilates, Part 1

The year I took intensive Pilates—and by intensive, I mean twice weekly private sessions with a borderline sadist—was actually a pivotal point for me, because it was the first time I learned to be fully present in my body. Prior to that, I had an exceptionally high pain threshold, which I thought was a good thing at the time. Now in retrospect, I can see it was merely a function (dysfunction?) of detachment from my physical form. As a child, I was not grounded and often crashed my shins and knees into low-lying furniture, because I was not rooted in my body. Pilates quickly made me aware of this and helped me learn to ground into my body.

I can recall a particular session on the Pilates Cadillac. That is seriously what they call it, because apparently its original name "Trap Table" wasn't good for sales. In this session, my tormentor, er—instructor fussed at me because I could not make one of my hips do what she was asking me to do. She demanded to know why I was so slow in following her instructions. I meekly explained to her that my body simply does not respond to instructions immediately.

After further discussion, I realized I was not operating inside my body the way I should. The verbal messages she gave me did not translate into immediate nerve firings—instead, my brain had to consciously process and translate the words, and then specifically relay an instructional message to that body part. Have you ever seen someone study their hands for a moment to figure out which is right and which is left? Yeah, it was kinda like that.

Would you like to see whether you're rooted in your body or not? Let's do a quick experiment. Stand up right now. Oops! Didn't mean for that to sound so militant! Pretty please, could you stand up now? Thanks, doll. Now raise your right leg and step it back. Left arm reaches over your head. Step the left leg back and lower the arm. Swing your left hip outward, then move your right shoulder back. Open your chest. Bring both arms up and behind your head. Okay, you're done; you can relax now and return to whatever position you were in before we interrupted you with this quick stretch break.

How quickly were you able to follow that sequence of instructions? Did it happen almost instantaneously as you were reading it, or did it take a second or two to register first?

Amy Scott Grant: Surviving Pilates, Part 2

Before I was rooted in my body—and I'm thinking specifically of the session where I first noticed it, when I was on the Trap Table—Pilates went a little something like this:

Pilates drill sergeant: "Rotate your left hip toward me."

Me, silently: Brain receives message, brain interprets message: which hip is left? Ah, that one. Brain thinks message toward left hip: "You there, rotate toward her." Hip talks to brain, "Who, me? What do you mean, rotate?" Brain thinks, then sends an image to hip: "Do it like this." Hip responds tentatively, then sends message back to brain, "Like this? This is really hard. Am I doing it right?" Brain doesn't know, because brain has no reference point for this new machine work.

Meanwhile, something like four seconds have passed, and the drill sergeant grows impatient. "What are you waiting for? Rotate your left hip toward me!"

The discussion that followed was rather eye opening for me. I soon realized why I had always been so slow at sports and yoga, why my posture was terrible, and why parts of my body felt downright weak and pathetic. My body-brain connection wasn't strong, which meant I couldn't physically react immediately, despite years of becoming quite adept at video games.

Pilates helped me to create that mind-body connection I had heard so many people talk about, and it prompted me to do heaps of clearing work around my body and my brain. If you've ever taken Pilates, then you know it's a ton of ab work. Every move in Pilates requires you to engage your abs, a habit I believe everyone deserves to develop. Engaging your abs instantly makes you stronger and more stable. Are you seeing the connection to the root chakra yet? Plus, strong abs help to stave off back problems, injuries, and misalignment.

But Pilates is not for everyone, so I'm not here to talk you into it. Yoga is awesome! While writing this book, I decided to start taking yoga classes again, to reignite more flexibility in this body. Today, yoga is practically a 31-flavors shop. You can choose from all sorts of varieties of yoga. Personally, I like hot yoga and restorative yoga, but it's very much a personal preference. The common thread among all types of yoga is the focus on the breath. Whenever you consciously focus on breathing, you are also grounding. The proper execution of yoga inherently requires grounding—yes, even those crazy inverted poses—so the two go hand-in-hand.

Martial Arts: Similarly, martial arts classes focus on the mind-body-spirit connection with a strong emphasis on being calm and centered. Many stances in martial arts begin with a feet-apart stable position, where the root chakra is "in position." Add to this the physical awareness of martial arts training, and you can see how these ancient disciplines involve quite a bit of grounding.

Breath Work

Oh, the choices abound with breath work! We could write a whole book on the powers of breath work, and maybe that will appear in some future edition of The Lightworker's Guide. For now, let's explore a few breathing methods for quick and easy grounding.

Deep breathing is a method you're likely familiar with. When we become anxious or stressed, our breathing naturally becomes shallow. The trouble is, shallow breathing fails to fill your lungs, leaving your cells under-oxygenated. Deep breathing delivers more oxygen to your cells, making you more capable of dealing with whatever is stressing you out in the first place.

Additionally, when you focus on deep breathing from your core—better yet, from the Earth's core—you quickly ground and relax. To breathe in from the Earth's core, simply imagine that you are reaching down into the Earth and pulling that energy into your body as you breathe deeply and mindfully. Remember the grounding cord? You can imagine you are breathing from the Earth's core, up your grounding cord, and into your body. Try it now and notice how instantly it grounds you.

A fun alternative to deep breathing is to sigh out your breath, a popular practice used by many yoga instructors. Simply breathe in deeply and then let out a long audible sigh as you exhale. Likewise, you can breathe out a specific word for grounding, such as "calm," "peace," "relax," etc.

Huna Breathing

Have you heard of Huna breathing? No, silly, there are no grass skirts and coconut bras involved. That's hula; this is Huna, although both originated in the same place. In Hawaiian, the word "huna" means secret, as it relates to the hidden wisdom and teachings. Huna breathing was thought to be able to create an altered state, which was basically a job requirement for the big Kahunas. Hey, look at that! "huna" is right there inside the word "Kahuna!"

Huna breathing is a rhythmic style of breathing that forces you to be mindful as you consciously count your breaths. Huna breath experts and teachers will likely be annoyed with the abbreviated and somewhat cavalier description we're about to deliver, but if you want to know all about Huna breathing, you're welcome to buy one of those expert's books. Because a quick online search will show you just how many contradictory teachings are out there on this subject. Hey, talk about your secret wisdom—even today it remains well-hidden!

Here's what you need to know to get started: Consider that there are four components to every breath: breathing in, holding that breath, breathing out, then pausing before the next breath. Sounds like a lot for something that your body manages to carry out instinctively and naturally, about a zillion times per day, right? . But the practice of Huna or Ha (also known as Huna Ha) breathing causes you to mindfully breathe, counting in this ratio: 1:1:2:1. Which means, if you breathe in for three counts, then you would hold for three counts, then breathe out for six counts, then hold for three counts. Basically, your exhalation is twice as long as your inhalation, which lasts as long as the hold and the pause. On each exhale, make a soft "haaaaaaaaa" sound for the full count.

Lamaze style breathing was originally designed to keep women in labor focused and relaxed during childbirth, as well as (allegedly) providing some degree of pain management. This can also have a grounding effect, as it is almost impossible not to engage your diaphragm when practicing the "he-he-hoooo" pattern: two short breaths out to the sound of "he" followed by a longer, relaxed exhalation to the sound of "hoooo."

These are just a few examples, but nearly any kind of focused breath work is effective in grounding, because it makes you more aware of your body while you activate your root chakra. Breath work is another excellent addition to face-to-face Lightworking sessions, as well as group work, workshops, retreats, etc.

Tapping into Animal Energy

If you're like Terry and you feel super connected to the animal kingdom, you'll love this method of grounding. Essentially, you choose an animal and then commune with it energetically. For example, if you've always admired lions, then you find ways to connect with the energy of the lion. You might:

- Visit your local zoo and spend time observing and/or photographing the lions.
- Research lions at the library or online.
- Buy a lion stuffed animal.
- Listen to Katy Perry's song "Roar"
- Create art depicting lions.
- Go see *The Lion King* at the theater.
- Channel Simba or Nala or Mufasa.
- Read up on the Native American legends and the mythology of this powerful creature.
- Start hanging out with Leos... careful there, just sayin'.
- Sponsor endangered big cats.
- Get a new haircut that resembles a shaggy mane.
- Practice roaring.
- Pick up a faux animal blanket for your sofa or bed.
- Etc.

You might think we're joking about some of these suggestions, but whatever the animal brings forth in you, these items and actions help to anchor that animal's energy and gifts in your mind by bringing physical representations of it into your space. There are countless ways to connect with animals, and doing so often has a grounding effect, especially for earthbound animals (as opposed to fish and birds). This is a fun and playful way to ground, so get ready to roar, baby, ROAR!

Terry Robnett: Me and My Animals

Animal grounding isn't just for pet therapy and service animals! Pets help us de-stress, heal, and ground. As you may or may not know, animals are very sensitive to energy fields. In fact, animals serve many roles when it comes to energy and the planet. Their energy fields are way more expansive than ours. Their energetic frequencies help to maintain the vibrational health on earth and all other living things. The animals are here to help us, believe it or not.

A lot of animals are empathic as well. This means that they take on the thoughts, feelings, and/or emotions of their surroundings, which is why a lot of them have a variety of mental, emotional, and physical issues themselves. I grew up around all kinds of animals. I had cats, dogs, chickens, bunnies, and birds. I lived in a neighborhood where my friends had horses, cows, goats, pigs, peacocks, reptiles, and other crazy animals. I could probably write a whole book about how animals have helped ground me.

There is just something about an animal that automatically and instantly brings you back to center. One of the most memorable stories I can share with you is about my grey angora cat named Ora. She had the most beautiful green eyes and long silky hair. She would sleep with me every night. She was my serenity. My comfort. My center. Isn't that what grounding is? All those things and more? Every time I would hold her, pet her, or she would lay with me, there would always be a sense of calm and genuine feelings of love and belonging. So many times, if I was in a bad mood (boy oh boy did I have a temper back then) or having a bad day, all it would take for me to shift that was to hold her and everything would be all right again.

Even now as a grown adult, I have birds, a tortoise, and a backyard full of wild animals that come to see me. Mainly because I feed them, but still. They are all very grounding and healing for me, except my cockatiel "Roxy," who is a total Diva to me because she only loves my husband.

Chanting and Toning

Although Pope Gregory I gets most of the credit for "Gregorian Chanting," experts say it was an anonymous group effort to create widespread use of chanting. The practice of chanting a repetitious rhythmic or sing-song phrase, without any accompanying music was virtually commonplace in Rome by the end of the eighth century. So suffice it to say, chanting is pretty damn old.

What should you chant for grounding? You can try just about anything, but keep your voice low and deep and relatively slow, as this is more aligned with the lower part of the body, and therefore, more likely to affect the lower chakras. You could chant "I am grounding now" and see how that feels. Or you might choose just one word, like "calm" or "safety." The single mystic syllable "om" is said to be the sound of the universe, so that's a good go-to for chanting.

What does chanting sound like? Here are a few examples: "Luke, I am your father," "nanny-nanny-boo-boo," and "owatta seelee goo siam." Try that last one out loud a few times. If none of those ring a bell, rent the movie *Monty Python and the Holy Grail* and pay close attention to the monks.

Toning works in a similar way, except you are playing with sounds as opposed to words. Simply take any sound, then pick a note and drag that sound out for about eight beats approximately; it's not an exact science, so do whatever feels good to you. Then take a breath and do it again. Every once in awhile, either change the sound or the note, or slide up or down mid-toning. You can tone the vowel sounds "ahhhh, ehhhh, eeeee, ohhhh, ooooo," or whatever you want, really. Just you wait 'enry 'iggins, just you wait.

Amy Scott Grant: Toning with Intention

A friend of mine introduced me to toning several years ago by sharing some audios a friend of hers had made. The idea is that as you listen to the recording, you tone along with her, matching your voice to hers. Well to be perfectly honest, that woman's voice grated on my last nerve, so after listening once or twice, I decided to just do it on my own. Then, in classic Amy style, I started to experiment and found a way to make toning even better. Here's what I discovered about toning:

You can produce excellent results when you tone a word. Okay, so maybe that technically becomes chanting. Split a hair, why don't you? As long as it works, do you really care what it's called? I chose a single-syllable word, although I've found two-syllable words work just as well, though it does slightly change the toning process and make it more chant-like. After I chose the word, I set an intention before I started toning. Here's how that played out:

The word I chose: wealth

I picked a low, deep, slow tone. I'm an alto, so feel free to adjust yours accordingly.

Then I set this intention to the Universe: As I tone the word "wealth," please align me with the energy of wealth.

Then I started toning. Weaaaaaaaaaaaaaaaaaaalth. I repeated that maybe a dozen times or so.

As it turns out, the churchgoing crowd is right about something: "When you sing, you pray twice." I found I could manifest a whole lot faster when toning a word, as compared to merely affirming that same word.

I repeated this toning process nightly just before bed over the course of a few weeks, and quickly noticed a shift. It wasn't just about bringing in more abundance; I was already doing that. I specifically wanted to access wealth. To me, that means being wise with money, letting money accumulate, increasing my net worth, and releasing all debt. I noticed an increase in my income once I started toning, and found money easier to handle with prudence, as well as to appropriately prioritize our investments, diversification, and the overall management of our money. Try it and watch what happens!

You could argue that toning is a form of breath work, and you'd probably be right about that. For sure, it has a calming and centering effect which naturally leads to grounding. If you are a person who likes to "do" and stay active, you may find toning to be easier and more satisfying than traditional meditation, since toning gives you something to "do" while you relax and focus.

Whether you call it chanting or toning or noisy breath work, we invite you to try this out for yourself and let us know what kind of results you get. You can share with us and our ever-growing Lightworkers' community here:

TheLightworkersGuide.com

Grounding Sounds

What is the sound of one person grounding? Grunting, chanting, and toning aren't the only sounds that can be effective for grounding. Consider the following options:

White noise. Soft static, babbling brooks, rainforest at night, what's your pleasure? It wasn't too long ago that a person had to purchase a special white noise machine to access the wonders of grounding sounds. Now you can easily take your pick of apps or CDs designed to relax and ground you with their soothing sounds, wherever you go.

Music. Different songs have different effects on different people, so when deciding whether or not a song is grounding for you, consider how you feel when you hear it. Songs that make you feel excited, like you want to stand up and dance, for example T-Swift's "Shake It Off," or songs that make you feel agitated, like you want to leap up and change the radio, such as "The Macarena," are not necessarily good grounding choices. But a song that calms and soothes you—including a song that may put you to sleep—is an excellent grounding tool. For some, this is a *style* of music like classical, jazz, or country; or a particular *artist* such as George Winston, Barenaked Ladies, or Enya; or a particular *album* like the Beatles' *White* album, Pink Floyd's *Dark Side of the Moon,* or the soundtrack of a movie or musical. You may even choose a particular song that carries special meaning for you. This would be considered a passive form of grounding, since all you typically have to do is put the song on and let the magic happen.

Other sounds. Nature sounds, animal sounds, wind chimes, fountains, certain musical instruments, playground sounds, perhaps even the sound of dishes being washed, especially if you're not the one having to wash them. Any sound that you find soothing and comforting can easily be incorporated as a grounding tool.

Scent-sational Grounding

What kinds of scents have a calming and relaxing effect on you? For some, it's warmer aromas, such as baked apples, toast, cinnamon, pumpkin, bread, ginger, etc. For others, earthy or musky scents like fresh cut grass, soil (think:

gardening), patchouli, sandalwood, pine, etc. do the trick. And for still others, it might be flower scents, like lavender, violet, rose, or vanilla. You can easily use your favorite scents of essential oils, aromatherapy, or candles as wonderful smelling grounding tools. Heck, even a scratch-and-sniff sticker or a scented lip balm would work. Remember those Mr. Sketch markers? The black one was always Amy's fave. Which is weird, since she doesn't eat licorice.

Good news: you don't have to apply essential oils directly to your body to access their powerful grounding effect. You can use a diffuser or dab a drop on something in your immediate environment, like a pillow or blanket or even your favorite pen. Do be careful though—like perfume, oils can stain certain fabrics. Terry has oil diffusers all around her home, and Amy often diffuses essential oils during retreats and in her home office. We invite you to experiment and see which scents in what kind of applications work best to create a grounding effect for you.

Terry Robnett: Grounding with the Light Inside

One of the coolest, but more advanced things I've learned, is how to crank up your light inside just like you would a light with a dimmer switch. You know what a dimmer switch is, right? You know that dial where the light switch allows you to make the light in the room super bright or super dim? So, let me tell you a quick story. Oh duh, this is a story (laughing out loud to myself).

Like most people, when I was first learning about being a Lightworker, I learned the basics of how to ground with the roots coming out of my feet into the ground like a tree... blah blah blah. I also learned how to protect myself in the bubble of light.

Okay, so just real quick let me touch a little on the light inside.

We all have a light inside of us. Like a light house or beacon in the night, or just like a water heater has a pilot light that is always on, this light inside has the ability to be as dim or as bright as you desire. Since most of us are unaware of our own personal light's existence, for the sake of this quick story, let me shed a little light. Hahaha. Get it? A little Light? I know, bad joke. Anyway, I guess you could equate it to a circuit board where we are all connected to a Divine platform and grounded to the earth as One. You are simply tapping into that grounded platform to enhance your light inside, just like you would turn on the lights in your home. As soon as you realize you are connected, you get a little crazy, turning all your lights on, right?

Well, me being me, I generally like to find and/or create bigger, better, faster, more streamlined ways of doing things. So what did I do? I started practicing, consistently utilizing, and teaching others the "light bulb with a dimmer switch" tool after a vision I had, showing me how it's done. This tool enables one to ground AND project your light inside, so far out into the Universe that it acts as a natural barrier for lots of things.

Intentionality

Often the simplest solution is the best, and the most frequently overlooked. At times, a clear and specific intention can be all you need to ground immediately. And we're not talking about a grand intention for where you want to go next in your life or what you wish to manifest; but rather, the simple intention of getting grounded.

This is a powerful tool for any Lightworker, because through the course of your Lightworking throughout your life, you will encounter many a soul who feels lost, distraught, stressed out, upset, and ungrounded. When you can simply intend that you are grounded and it happens, you can then open a space for grounding to occur for the other person who is seeking your help. Think of this as putting on your own oxygen mask on the airplane before assisting another. But, you know. Without the imminent threat of a plane crashing down.

This intention for grounding can be as quick and easy as settling into your body, becoming aware of your intent to ground, or just being present and showing up, no matter what is going on around you.

Ashleigh Farrell, MSN, RN: Kites and Hurricanes

How does one stay connected and sane when they are spread thin and scattered? I'm the proud wearer of many hats. I'm a mom of four beautiful wild children, a wife, a business owner, an educator, a nurse, the list goes on. I'm pulled in a million different directions at any given moment of the day and there is never a spare moment for "me" time. It may seem impossible to center yourself amidst chaos but reflection has taught me that the best way to remain sane in such an environment is to stay present and embrace the crazy, knowing that this too shall pass.

I stay grounded by showing up and participating wholeheartedly in life. I jump in with both feet and I ride the waves rather than fighting the current. Life comes in seasons, while some may be intense, others are mundane. Right now, I'm in a very chaotic and crazy season full of diapers, car seats, school lunches, deadlines, and bills, trying to be everything to everyone. However, I know this is fleeting and it will go by quicker than I can imagine. Likely quicker than I want it to at the end of the day.

It's as if I'm holding a bunch of kites and some days the breeze is calm and gentle and the kites fly around beautifully like they're dancing in a perfectly orchestrated performance. Other days, there are hurricane winds and those things are blowing around like maniacs while I hold on for dear life and people are looking at me like I'm insane. They're thinking why the heck is this lady trying to fly kites in a hurricane instead of quitting and walking inside a calm and quiet building? Yet I just stand out there in the wind and fly my kites because I know that one day, there may not be a breeze. That is the only certainty of life. One day the curtain call is up, and I will never regret a single day standing out in the hurricane with my kites. After all, those winds are the richness of my life.

I was begrudgingly imparted with this valuable life wisdom upon losing my father to cancer. The primary message I walked away with was to take the good times with the bad and soak up every last moment of this time we have here. The essence of life is not to endure it but rather to enjoy it in all of its complicated glory, the beauty and the warts, before our time is up. So if you ever see a woman standing in a hurricane flying kites, that's me, staying sane by showing up to my life no matter what it has in store for me.

In the next chapter, we'll delve into how to create your own grounding tools and methods. But first, why not take a few minutes to complete your Food for Thought?

Chapter 4 Food for Thought: who wants seconds?

1. Which, if any, of the active grounding methods in this chapter seem most appealing to you?

2. Take a minute to think, then list all the active grounding methods you now use. Recognizing them here can reinforce their value in your mind, helping you remember to employ them more often.

3. Referring back to the spaces you listed back in Chapter 2 Food for Thought, how can you incorporate more active grounding methods and tools to make these spaces feel more grounded?

4. Which active grounding methods in this chapter feel most unfamiliar to you? List them all, then circle two that you are willing to try out this week. Write down whatever results you experience.

Chapter 5: Creating Your Own Grounding Methods

Yes! You can create your own grounding tools, and there are many ways to do this. And as a Lightworker, when you create your own grounding methods, you are further increasing the value you bring to those you're helping through Lightworking.

Mind you, nobody said you had to go out and invent your own grounding methods when there are so many perfectly good ones right here inside this book. This chapter explores some ideas and jumping off points for creating your own grounding tools, should you have the desire to. It's not a requirement, for Lightworkers or otherwise. However, you might wish to create your own, in order to make it feel more personal, to more fully use what's already in your space, to improve upon an existing grounding tool or method, or just because you like to be different. We see you, Unicorn!

Some grounding methods are created through divine inspiration, while others are created out of necessity. Perhaps the simplest way to create your own grounding methods is with your *intention*.

Intention carries a lot of weight, and you can start right now by adding an intention of *grounding* to items that are already within your reach. Here are some specifics.

Sensorial Perspectives

One of the easiest ways to start creating your own grounding tools is to begin with the five senses. Which of the following do you feel most connected to right now?

- Sight
- Sound
- Taste
- Touch
- Smell

An alternative way to approach this is to ask yourself: which of the five senses above are you most sensitive to?

Amy Scott Grant: Ooooo That Smell

For me, the sense I'm most aware of is smell. It is difficult for me to focus or relax in the midst of an overpowering smell. I have been known to step out of an elevator or alter my grocery aisles route in order to avoid someone with overbearing perfume, or who reeks of cigarette smoke. Strong, unpleasant smells make me agitated and edgy, which can cause me to become ungrounded.

Now take that sensitive sense and create a grounding tool for it. For example, in the winter, Amy could create a grounding tool out of a scarf by spraying it with her own perfume, or shpritzing it with a bit of diluted essential oil (cinnamon or peppermint, perhaps). That way, if she finds herself in an unpleasant-smelling situation, she can pull the scarf up over her nose and breathe in a scent that she finds comforting and grounding.

See how easy this is?

Jennifer Blumenthal: The Rebel's Guide to Grounding

I've always been a bit of a rebel. Not because I wanted to be different or buck authority, but because, more often than not, what "they" tell me to do doesn't work for me. (Believe me, I've tried!) So I continue to search for my own way of doing things that work for me. Maybe you feel this way too. For years, I grounded like "they" told me to: send roots from your feet into the earth… send a golden thread from your core down into Gaia… put your bare feet in the grass and your hands in the dirt, they said. Don't get me wrong, I do all those things and they feel lovely, but they don't make me feel "grounded"—at least, not by themselves.

Being truly grounded, for me, is when I'm plugged into my unique source of Soul nourishment. Being grounded clears the static within me and opens the channel wide to receive divine inspiration so that energy can flow through me without getting stuck. Being grounded in this way clears the path for manifesting and receiving, and creates a feeling of flow in the moment. I know when I'm grounded because I feel connected to Source, my energy settles, I feel content, and yet I also feel inspired and energized at the same time. Inspiration pours in and I suddenly know what I am supposed to do. Distractions fall away and my focus sharpens. A sense of ease comes in and I can feel movement—like that moment when a plane tops the clouds and the ride becomes quiet and smooth.

That's how I know I'm truly grounded.

What does it feel like for you? The trick is that nobody can tell you how to plug into your unique source of Soul nourishment. You'll know it when you feel it, and the only way to find it is to experiment. So I invite you to take a journey to discover what nourishes you. Find the practices and rituals that take you to that place of feeling connected in every direction where inspiration flows through you until you know.

The practices that ground me include some combination of:
- *conversations with Spirit through oracle cards*
- *doodling*
- *drawing mandalas*
- *gardening*
- *talking with trees*
- *finger painting*
- *journaling*
- *wrapping sticks with colored thread*
- *earthing*
- *filling my body with energy from both earth and sky*
- *energy clearing*
- *my Moon Wishing practice*
- *fire ceremonies*
- *feather walks*

Your practices might include some of these as well as hiking, yoga, meditation, star gazing, dancing, chanting, singing, cartwheels, or anything else that brings you home to yourself and plugs you in. The secret lies in giving yourself enough time in your practices to move beyond the mind and let your Soul nourishment take over. So, fellow rebel, what's your unique recipe for grounding? Only you can find it for yourself, and when you do, you'll know because it will make you feel like you've found your Self and you are home.

If you're a very visual person, you can add nature scenes to your surroundings or put some nature scenes on your phone, tablet, and laptop, so you'll have visually comforting and grounding sights wherever you go.

Begin to listen for soothing sounds that you can record or purchase and carry with you on your smartphone. This might include a white noise app, a recording of a loved one's voice (careful, stalking is a slippery slope), or the crooning cadence of Deepak Chopra. Ahhhh, isn't his voice simply intoxicating? Dontcha just love the way he says "welcome" and it comes out sounding more like "villkem." Several of Amy's books are available as audiobooks because many people find it comforting to be read to, and since Amy is a naturally grounded person, it follows that many people find her voice to be soothing and comforting. She doesn't personally get it, but hey, whatever floats your boat.

Claim Your Elements

Why not create your own grounding tools and methods from the elements? In feng shui, the five elements are wood, fire, earth, metal, and water. In Buddhism, the five elements are earth, water, fire, wind, and *void* (think: heaven and stuff beyond the physical realm). Which of the following do you feel most connected to right now?

- Earth
- Wood
- Water
- Fire
- Metal
- Wind
- Void

Earth is naturally grounding, so you really can't go wrong with any choices there. In addition to the "earth" section in this book, you may find things that specifically connect you to earth. A few examples include: a bottle of sand from your favorite beach, a pebble you picked up during a walk with your loved one, pottery you've made or painted yourself, etc.

In feng shui, wood represents new growth and expansion. If wood and trees feel the most grounding to you, you could use intention to create grounding tools out of your back deck, anything bamboo, house plants, that fake ficus tree in your foyer, etc.

Water is not necessarily a grounding element. However, the use or observation of water can be extremely grounding. Think about how it feels to listen to waves crashing into the beach, a babbling brook, or the sound of rain. How calm do you feel when you gaze into a beautiful fountain or a well-kept fish tank? How relaxing is a hot soak or a bubble bath? When Amy was a kid, she had one of those contained water toys with the colored liquid that dripped down in slow spiraling patterns, and she literally spent hours watching its calming fluidity. Ever been camping? There's nothing quite as satisfying as a long, hot shower when you return home. Water can be grounding, depending on how you use it and how you feel about it. A person who once nearly drowned is going to have a very different experience on a jet ski as compared to a person who grew up on boats as a child.

Terry Robnett: Shower Chamber

I don't know about you, but my shower is one of the most sacred spaces and places in the house. Like most people, I have a routine, but I think mine is extraordinary since I refer to it as my "shower chamber." When I say routine, I mean that everyone has their typical step-by-step they do from the moment they get in the shower, like wash their hair first then their face and so on, to the moment they get out of the shower. If you pay attention, I am certain you will agree that you take a shower the same way every time.

94

For me, it's different because I intend and incorporate the actual washing of my physical self with the re-centering, healing, and cleansing of the mind, body, and soul. What makes the shower chamber the perfect place is that I am usually always alone, which means no outside distractions. It's quiet, which is perfect for meditation and clarity. Nobody bothers me... for the most part. I typically get to spend the time I need to get 'er done.

When I get in the shower, I first let the water touch my head and down the rest of my body. As I begin to wash from head to toe, I envision all the dense dark energies attempting to cause sickness, illness, disease, and more being easily lifted away from the body and washed down the drain, so it can be absorbed into the core of the earth. Through intention, the mind, body, and soul are restored to an optimally balanced and healthy state of being.

Fire can be extremely grounding as long as you feel safe around it. How long have you spent mesmerized by a roaring campfire or a candle's flicker? Time seems to slip into oblivion when we are captivated by controlled fire. You can see how this would not be the case for someone who is afraid of fire, or someone who has experienced a loss due to fire. If you find fire to be grounding and calming, you might designate your favorite candle as "the grounding candle," or intend that smoked items such as salmon, salt, cigars, etc., create a grounding effect for you. You could intend that your grill is grounding, and every time you fire up the grill it grounds everyone nearby as well as the food you're cooking on it. Brings new meaning to the phrase "grillin' and chillin'," right Bobby Flay?

Metal is not typically a grounding element. This is why feng shui cautions against metal bedposts and headboards, as these are said to impede a good night's rest. But that doesn't mean metal objects are off-limits as grounding tools for you!

Here are a few examples of **how Amy uses metals in grounding:**

My dear friend Suzanne gave me a sterling silver ring of spirals for my birthday one year. I wear it almost daily, and it has a deeply calming effect on me.

Likewise, I wear hoop earrings nearly every day. I own all different sizes and textures—and I do have other shapes and styles of earrings—but the hoops are most often my go-to, and have been for years. The circle is such a powerful spiritual symbol of oneness and infinity, no wonder it grounds me naturally.

Finally, there's a huge chunk of metal in my life, which grounds me every time I use it. I have never been particularly fond of driving, until a couple of years ago when I bought a Prius. We call him "Kevin" and I don't know what it is about this car, but I feel amazing every time I get behind the wheel. Kevin makes me feel safe, calm, and relaxed, even while in traffic or when someone cuts me off. Hard to imagine a car named after a minion could do all that, right?

Like metal, wind is not a particularly grounding element. However, you might designate grounding elements from wind chimes, prayer flags, ceiling fans, or any wind-related object.

Are you beginning to see how grounding tools and methods can be so very personal, based on what makes YOU feel calm and centered?

"Void" has sort of an ethereal quality to it, making it very un-earth like. However, symbols of spirit, thought, heaven, sky, and creativity could certainly be deemed grounding items, if your intention is to make them so. Perhaps you'll find yourself grounded by images of the Ascended Masters, angels, the sky, a vision board, the Spiritual Ass Kicker's Discovery Deck, or other oracle decks.

Terry Robnett: Momma Moon Energy

The moon is not just the moon. It is another source of great energy and power. Over time I have developed a great relationship with the moon. We are like besties. We talk all the time. If I am being honest, I actually do most of the talking, sometimes sharing, and other times just venting.

Momma moon has her own special energy that pierces through your third eye passing through your whole body and out through your feet to the core of the earth. This instantaneously grounds you and takes all dense energy with it. It is akin to a lightning rod going through your body. No pain of course. Sliver moons are fun because it looks like it's smiling. Half-moons appear to be playing hide and seek, and full moons are the best because they seem bigger, closer, and way more powerful. It is during the full moon that you want to lay out all of your crystals to cleanse and recharge.

Did it ever cross your mind that since the moon cleanses and restores crystals, it could do the same for you too? Crystals are made up of energy and are very grounding. You too are made up of energy and are very connected. So next time you sit outside, look for momma moon and introduce yourself. Talk to her and bond so that you too can have a new bestie to share with, vent to, and solve all the problems of the world.

Remember, you're not limited by your senses or the elements—these are just examples to help you jump start your own ideas. After all, if we tell you what to use, then you're not creating your own methods and tools, are you? Not that you have to, of course. We're simply offering options. You can certainly serve your Lightworking duties quite well using any combination of the methods we've explained in this book.

And by the same token, it doesn't make you an overachiever if you want to create your own grounding methods. We invite you to do whatever feels most optimal for you.

Will Hale: Simple Harmony

There is a commonly held false belief that complicated issues need complicated solutions. You can prove to yourself this is a lie by learning this simple skill right now in the next few minutes. The best way I have found to get grounded and restore harmony is to feel my physical heartbeat. How simple is that! Don't take my word for it. Try it now! Can you feel your heart beating? It is surprising how often people have a hard time feeling their heart beat even though it is a constant force in our bodies. It is common to associate feeling our heartbeat with fear or overexertion. What if feeling your heartbeat could be your closest companion, a gentle natural reminder that you are alive, you are safe, feeling rhythm and harmony in every situation?

There is nothing metaphorical, emotional, or energetic related to this heart grounding method. The entire focus is direct observation of our physical heartbeat. The countless hidden benefits of this practice are as simple as not having to understand how electricity works to turn on a light switch. It can be easy to feel your heartbeat with your hand on your chest while holding a deep breath. If it is still hard to feel your heartbeat, you can do twenty jumping jacks. You will start to feel your heart beat!

Amazing things happen when you add awareness of your breath with the awareness of your heartbeat. Try breathing in rhythmically eight heartbeats and breathe out eight heartbeats. Practice adding three rhythmic breaths to your daily routine for the next week. With a week of consistent practice, you will begin to personally experience the value of being able to feel your heartbeat anytime, anywhere. The synchronized rhythm of our heartbeat, breath, and mental focus can greatly amplify the experience of harmony and balance in your life. This simple state of being supports increased relaxed confidence and more effective results in our daily activities.

Action triggers are a great way to establish a new skill. You can build a reliable habit of feeling your heartbeat by pre-deciding to focus your attention on your heart related with a specific task. A few examples would be: feeling your heart as soon as you get in the shower or when you get in the car before starting the engine, before eating, or while the computer is booting up. A stable grounded heart breath can easily become your natural everyday breath. Once you find your balance, you will be able to take off the training wheels and trust the invisible force that beats your heart to be in charge. Enjoy the pleasant process of getting to know your heart. Like swimming, feeling your heart is a lifelong skill you will never lose and could save your life.

Try creating your own grounding tools from music, images, objects, totems and talismans, feelings, chants, affirmations, jewelry, clothing, food, accessories, art, and even a pendulum. This chapter is rather short because it literally is just that easy. What's your favorite way to ground? Share it with us while you connect with all types of Lightworkers from many walks of life here in our Lightworker's Guide private community:

TheLightworkersGuide.com

Why not take a minute now to join, before you move on to the Food for Thought?

Chapter 5 Food for Thought: finger lickin' good!

1. How do you feel about the idea of creating your own grounding methods? Have you ever done this before? If not, are you willing to give it a shot? Why or why not?

2. What are the characteristics of your ideal grounding method? For example, you might want it to be: totally portable, inexpensive, luxurious, personalized, warm and comforting, useful indoors or outdoors, passive, etc.

3. Which of the five senses are you most sensitive to? Which are you most drawn to? Do you feel inspired to create a grounding tool based on this? What ideas come up?

4. Which of the elements are you most drawn to? Do you feel inspired to create a grounding tool based on this? What ideas come up?

Chapter 6:

Grounding for Lightworkers

As a Lightworker, it is essential to remain calm and steady, so that you're not swept away in the massive energy shifts that surround us. On any given day, you could be exposed to negative entities, unresolved conflicts, strong emotions and physical reactions, toxic energy, energy vampires, etc. Empaths are even more susceptible to the effects of these. Grounding helps prevent you from taking on any of these burdens of your clients.

Additionally, as a Lightworker, you can be of greatest service when your own energy is stable and centered. This creates a safe space for those with whom you are working. Being grounded as a Lightworker also helps to create a more satisfying, more stable spiritual business for yourself.

Terry Robnett: Creating a Column of Light

Through one's evolutionary journey, it is a given that you grow and change and elevate in all aspects of your life, right? Grounding is just one of those many aspects. Yet it is something we tend to dismiss early on. I have learned over the decades through my own growth and elevation that grounding can occur naturally in a gamut of ways. I have also discovered that what works for one does not necessarily work for another. In case you hadn't noticed, there is no one size fits all. The most recent and very successful way I have learned is through what I call "column of light."

Knowing that I am a channel through which Divine Love, Light, and Healing flows, I use a column of light as a way to achieve ongoing and successful grounding. How this works is that I see myself in, within, and surrounded by a very bright white (almost blinding) column of light that comes from the infinite Universe. If you're a visual person I guess you could equate it to being ground level inside an elevator shaft with massive floodlights shining down in it (insert thinking face).

Anyway, while in this column of light, I say out loud or using my inside voice, "I am open to be One with the Divine Light. I am honored to be a channel through which Divine Light flows to and through me." As I visualize this event in my mind's eye, I can see very clearly how and when I become one, connected... "grounded." I then set the intention to remain continuously grounded within the White Light. Staying connected. Just like you would plug something into an electrical outlet in your wall. It is at that point I can see a halo that expands from the core of my being expressing infinitely outwards, now acting as a natural protection barrier. Hence no more protection bubble needed (yes!) This modality, "column of light," covers many things to include: Grounding, Protection, Healing, Rejuvenation, Love, Bliss, and so much more. SO GET GROUNDED!

Here are some of the times **when grounding is most useful for Lightworkers, specifically:**

- just before a remote or in-person one-on-one session
- before working on yourself
- before engaging in energy work of any kind
- before group work
- at the beginning of a session, with your client/student included in the grounding process. This may or may not include an intention setting as well.
- after a session on yourself or others
- when heavy emotions or deep healing work come to the surface
- grounding your space each day, before each session, or after Lightworking is completed for the day
- grounding a space before, during, and after group work
- before signing a new client
- before a strategy call with a potential client
- just before asking for the sale
- before creating any kind of online collateral for your Lightworking, for example: social media, promotions or offers, writing website copy, articles, Facebook lives, podcasts, etc.
- before writing, which may or may not be channeled, as it relates to Lightworking, such as books, articles, emails, sales pages, calls to action, webinar scripts, pay per click ads, etc.
- when your client is upset
- when you are upset
- when you are having trouble concentrating
- when your client seems all over the place
- when your client seems distracted and can't focus on your work with them
- grounding your electronics; especially if you use these electronics to conduct your Lightworking business; for example, your phone or laptop

- before a difficult conversation that might involve firing a client, telling someone you can no longer work with them, asking for a past due payment, delivering bad news, etc.

As you can see, grounding can become a huge and integral part of any Lightworker's day. Sure, it seems like a long list, but remember what you've learned so far in this book. Grounding can be quick, easy, and even automatic. This is why it's important to set up your Lightworking space to support you with grounding. Adding grounding methods as part of your Lightworking systems and processes will help you remain even more steady.

But what happens if you forget to ground?

Melissa Valdellon: Energy Work Was Depleting Me

When I committed to the journey of becoming a lightworker, I was able to participate in my first retreat and practice performing energetic healing work on others for the first time ever. I remember feeling so excited and nervous and overwhelmed, wondering if what I was doing was making any difference at all. At one point in the retreat, we were told to practice with a partner. So my partner and I went to another room to do our work, and I ended up leading her on a meditation that definitely helped her release multiple layers of guilt and pain, so much so that she was happy and rejuvenated after our session and left to take a walk on the grounds afterward. On the other hand, I was energetically spent. I needed to get into bed and take a nap to re-charge. It wasn't until after the big group got together for a debrief that I realized that in such similar sessions, I was depleting my own energy reserves because that's all I knew to do to get the healing work done for another person.

After recognizing that pattern, I really took to heart the importance of grounding before and during a session with others. In connecting with the earth, I'm able to draw up earth's limitless energy supply and channel that to help in clearings and healings for others without needing to tap into my own energy. As a result, the clearings and healings go deeper, integrations and shifts don't take as long, and both client and I feel energized at the end. As long as I stay firmly grounded, I've noticed that I'm no longer exhausted after a single session, and can now hold longer sessions for multiple people.

If you feel drained after giving energy work, you can bet it's because you don't have adequate grounding and self-care in place. In order to keep your energy strong, and to prevent burnout, it is essential that you take care of your own body, mind, and spirit, and grounding is a key element of your self-care. The best way to avoid feeling drained after *receiving* energy work is by drinking plenty of fresh water. This helps the body to process its way through whatever has just been released, not unlike a physical detox. Sure, sometimes a nap is necessary after receiving energy work, but if you feel like you need a nap every time you give energy work or healing, then it's time to up your self-care ante.

Kim Illingworth: Self Care for Grounding

It has been a process for the Universe to get my attention and show me that I am a lightworker. I have become a Reiki master and am currently learning to teach yoga. I take as many classes and read as many books and articles as I can on energy and helping to heal people.

I am in recovery from alcoholism. That being said, after I learned from two Reiki teachers and was attuned to Reiki at least 4 times, I still didn't feel like I "had" it. In order to truly feel like I could help others with their energy, I had to be grounded and make sure I was high vibrating. This is how I finally got grounded and felt ready to share my skills with others.

First, I had to quit drinking. I am not speaking to anyone who has no issues with alcohol or drugs and can drink like a normal person. For me, alcohol was sapping my power, that's the only way I can explain it. I was also smoking cigarettes occasionally and just eating like crap and not doing yoga. I was in a cycle of not taking care of myself. I was putting things into my body that were "low vibrating." The results were depression, physical and mental pain, and just plain disappointment in myself. I did not feel worthy to help others when I couldn't even help myself.

It has been a journey of letting go of things. Once I stopped drinking and smoking and got back into yoga, things really started changing. I started to eat higher vibrating foods, I stopped watching negative shows and the news. I let go of heavy toxic relationships and I felt lighter both physically and mentally. Then I began to feel my own power. I started doing Reiki on friends. They gave me feedback and seemed to be able to feel my Reiki. Since then, I have only continued to get better at being the lightworker I feel called to be.

Now I am not condemning having a glass of wine or a cocktail—for me, I didn't have control over my drinking, and that's why I felt weak and not worthy. Once I started "self care" and treated myself with the love I have for others, that was when I could step into my role as lightworker. I was grounded by self care. Try it, you will become all you were meant to be and the world will benefit from you starting with yourself.

We could likely write an entire book called "The Lightworker's Guide to Self Care"—and perhaps that will appear at some point in this series—but for now, consider these tips:

- **Make yourself a priority.** There will never be enough time "left over" for you to practice self-care. Set a powerful example for your clients, your friends, your family, and everyone who knows you by prioritizing your own well-being.

- **Listen to your body and honor what it's telling you.** If alcohol makes you feel crappy, honor that and scale back your consumption. If you love pizza but it gives you horrible indigestion, have it less often. When you do have it, eat only the very best and don't settle for less. If you hate greens but you know your body craves them, work 'em into a smoothie or try a powdered greens option. If you're tired, rest. If you're achy, go have an Epsom soak. Everything else will still be there tomorrow. Listen to your body and honor its requests.

- **Create the most amazing space you possibly can for your Lightworking.** Create the space **you** want, not the space you think future someday clients might want. When you feel amazing in your space, you will find it easier to be fully present and purposeful and to perform at your very best.

- **When the Lightworking is complete, let it go and walk away.** The Universe does not need you meddling around in what might happen after a session. Do your best, and then let the Universe take the reins. This will allow you to be fully present in other areas of your life: as a spouse, a parent, a sibling, a neighbor, a friend. This will also allow you to fully enjoy the other things in life you love most, which incidentally, is another powerful form of self-care.

- **Charge what you're worth and don't apologize or rationalize it.** Too many Lightworkers are charging too little or nothing at all for their services, and then wondering why they feel exhausted and overextended by the end of the day. If this is difficult for you, then continue working on your self-worth, as this is also a part of self-care. If you choose not to charge at all, we strongly encourage you to create some kind of even exchange of energy, in order to maintain balance. Perhaps trading with another healer or Lightworker, or bartering services, or trading in some other fashion. There's a big difference between giving generously from your heart vs. being taken advantage of as a doormat. We'll talk more about "lopsided trades" and how to ground your barters in the next chapter.

- **Set and stick to boundaries.** A one-hour session must end within 60 minutes, not 75 or 90. This takes practice, but when you commit to ending on time, you will soon notice how much more smoothly and efficiently your sessions run. Amy works miracles in 15-minute Lightning Quick Clarity sessions, and because she books them back to back, running long is not an option. Her clients love these quick and powerful sessions! If Amy can accomplish this much in fifteen minutes, surely any Lightworker can complete whatever is optimal within sixty.

  Boundaries are important, not only for Lightworkers, but for the clients we serve. You're not doing anyone any favors by letting them walk all over you, as this will only leave you depleted and less able to serve others. You must be strong and stick to your boundaries, or else your Lightworking practice will suffer. This is a very effective form of self-care!

If You Get Triggered in a Session

Most Lightworkers have gotten "triggered" in a session at some point in their experience. When you first start out as a Lightworker, it can be difficult to maintain your composure in certain situations. For example, you may have experienced:

- You've just delivered a clear message from Source but then the person you're working with says "no, that can't be right."
- The client relates a gut-wrenching story and this stirs a strong emotional response within you. This happens often with empaths, especially early on, and it's not unusual for empaths to cry or become very emotional upon hearing the more difficult experiences of their clients.
- The person asks for help with an issue you haven't yet resolved for yourself. This can create feelings of self-doubt, anxiety, fear, worthiness, a sense of not being ready yet, wanting to hide or change the subject, etc.
- The client shares something shocking to you, and you can't help but feel judgmental, which is often immediately followed by feelings of guilt for being so "judgy."
- The client is clearly distracted and not fully present during your session.
- The person challenges you, demonstrates a lack of confidence in your skills, questions your authority, or otherwise sparks feelings of inadequacy in you.
- You feel a sudden onset of pain or physical discomfort, which didn't exist prior to the session. In most cases, this doesn't belong to you, but this happens often to empaths and clairsentients.
- You draw a blank, hit a wall, receive no info, don't trust the information you're getting, or otherwise don't know how to proceed.

- The other person shuts down and tries to bail from the session, when you are clear there's more work to be done.
- The client says he/she doesn't feel this is working and says they want to stop working with you.
- Your doorbell rings, your phone suddenly blows up with texts, your kid's school calls, you see a spider, the dog starts barking, your computer crashes, or any other sudden and immediate disturbance in your environment.

There are countless other reasons why you could become ungrounded during a session, but the *reason* is far less important than your *reaction* to it. The immediate goal is not to avoid ever becoming ungrounded, but rather, to get proficient at quickly noticing when you're not grounded and taking immediate steps to reground. Seek progress over perfection.

Melissa Valdellon: Better Than Shields or Bubbles

Being around emotionally charged people, crowds, or situations used to be so overwhelming, I'd actively work to minimize finding myself in such situations. I'd do things like go to the grocery store and run errands early in the morning before most people were awake, park far away from building entrances so I wouldn't have to deal with parking rage, or hide in my office when there were angry or upset customers around.

Early in my lightworker path, I learned about and ended up using various energetic shields and bubbles to minimize others' effects on me, and that worked—some of the time. When I could predict that I'd be finding myself in an ungrounded, uncertain situation, I knew to get myself grounded and centered so that I could set my shields in place.

Doing so worked wonders in deflecting a lot of the (often negative) energy going around. But then there were the times when people would suddenly get triggered into outbursts or I'd find myself unwittingly in a charged area, and I found I had trouble grounding anywhere near good enough to even begin creating and bringing up any energetic shields. In these instances, I'd find myself spending more time and energy trying to create shields that didn't last very long or didn't work at all because I was that ungrounded myself.

Somewhere along the way of realizing how ineffective all this effort of shielding was for me, I realized that simply the act of grounding firmly and strongly was enough for me to actually deflect any ungrounded energy from my space. What's even better is that the more I stay grounded and centered myself, I find myself coming across very few ungrounded people (or they become grounded shortly after coming into my space) and I can handle myself pretty well in crowds now, too. For the situations where I still occasionally run into ungrounded people or crowds now, staying focused on remaining grounded myself has been enough to shift the energy around me, and I don't have to think about creating shields or barriers anymore. So now, it's all a matter of staying grounded all the time, every day as much as I can—picturing my roots and some steel rods connecting from my hips deep into the earth and reinforcing that image every time I start noticing I'm not feeling like myself. I just stay grounded, and that's enough.

You can use any of the methods in this book when you notice you are ungrounded, but if it happens during a session, here are a few ways to create some space so you can take the time to ground yourself, your physical area, and/or your client:

- **Speak up.** For example, you could say, "Let's just take a minute to get grounded," or "Let's pause for a moment, I'm going to ground the energy now."

- **Bow out.** If you're on the phone, you might say, "I'm going to put you on hold for just a minute now." Then put down the phone and step out of the room to regroup and ground. If you're doing the work face-to-face, you can say, "I'm going to step out now for just a minute. You stay here and take three deep breaths, and I will be right back." We often think we need to explain ourselves when in reality, no explanation whatsoever is necessary. When you return to the call or the room, you can start by saying, "There. I needed to ground the energy so we could continue." That's it, it really is that simple.

- **Be still.** Whether in person or over the phone, you can take as much time as you need by simply announcing it. "I'm going to be silent for a few minutes, so I can [check in with your energy/connect with your Highest Self/talk to your guides/etc.] now. For now, you can simply focus on your breathing." This is the best option you could use if you ever get "stuck" in a session or feel you don't know what to do next. When you create the expectation of "for a few minutes" it helps them relax since there's nothing for the other person to do for the next few minutes. Rarely does it take that long, but it's better to say "for a few minutes" and have it take one minute, than to say "for one minute" and have it take five. Speaking of "take five," check out this super effective technique of Terry's.

Terry Robnett: Take Five

I call this "Take 5" because it allows you to clear on the fly, once you get the hang of it. This is definitely a more advanced technique. You can ground and clear wherever and whenever (working, driving, shopping, watching TV, etc.). As soon as you are faced with and can identify something (energy, attitude, unpleasant feeling, etc.) that is heavy/dense in nature, that is your cue to clear it. So take a few seconds to ground yourself and connect to source to allow a wide-open channel for clearing and receiving. The more you do this, the better and quicker you get and the more you can clear on the fly.

First, be willing to see your stuff! This helps to identify the dense energy that you intend to clear.

Be willing to change.

Be willing to see if you really want the reality you are choosing. Choose for love and you get more love.

Be willing to live in truth.

Then clear that density and old stuff.

REMEMBER, only live in the energies you wish in the future.

Once you are willing, you're ready to clear.

Now you need to connect to the light. You can request back up or support by connecting to your higher self, your guides, the Angels, etc. Take a deep breath and feel the energy of this light pulsating and starting to flow into you. Allow this light to start flowing into your crown chakra. Feel this light filling up your head, your eyes, your face. Feel this light flowing into your neck and your shoulders. This light is a source of relaxation and peace of mind. Feel this light filling into your chest, your heart, behind your shoulder blades. Let this light move down your arms and into your fingertips. Feel this light sourcing you and allow it into your belly, your back and into your hips. Breathe in. Allow this light to smooth out your energy fields. Feel this light bathe away all the stress and worry as it moves down your hips into your thighs, into your knees,

113

into your calves, and out your feet. From your hip area and root chakra, sense a steady stream of energy moving into the center of the planet. This is grounding it to you. Connect where you feel the happiest.

Any energies you desire to clear and release now you can let go of into the ground and/or the light. The earth loves you and completely supports you. Take a deep breath and feel how much the earth supports you. FEEL the light envelop you. FEEL yourself being a part of the Light.

Next, you use clearing statements like these:

Uncreate it - unplugging it from first moment you created it.

Delete it - across all time, dimensions, space, reality.

Destroy it - taking all the energy impulses out of your stories holding all energy in place.

Clear it - freeing the darkness creating a clean space.

Transmute it - changing the make up from dense to light.

And just so ya know, you can only delete falsehoods, <u>never truth</u>, because truth only gets more real. As mentioned before, Truth is Light in nature, whereas untruth is heavy and dense in nature. So in order to identify which is which, just practice everything you say by asking does this feel true and light?

So let's say you want to clear your dense feelings towards your mom. You will connect to the Pure Divine Blissful Light with a clear, open, and receiving, mind, body, and soul then you will say:

"I identify and acknowledge this dense energy that has presented itself as a negative feeling towards my mom, and I

114

choose now to uncreate it, delete it, and destroy it across all time, dimensions, space, and reality." Then ask: "What would it take to clear and transmute it and everything in the way of that; all energy, all vows and contracts, all spells and everything else that may be supporting that, PLEASE PLEASE PLEASE, UNCREATE IT, DELETE IT, AND DESTROY IT ACROSS ALL TIME DIMENSIONS SPACE AND REALITY."

It's always good to say it at least 3 times but even better 3-5 times just to lock it in with purpose and meaning.

You can do this all day every day for every little and big thing that comes up for you that feels dense and/or heavy in nature and you WILL see a difference, I PROMISE.

Here's the down and dirty:
  1. *Identify the dense heavy energy/feeling.*
  2. *Take a deep breath or two or three.*
  3. *Ground and connect as noted above.*
  4. *Clear as noted above.*

That is how you Take 5.

Grounding Your Practice

Whether your Lightworking is currently a practice or a full-fledged business, there is great benefit in grounding it. Grounding your practice will help you to feel energized and enlivened during sessions and it will build your confidence. Grounding your business helps with every aspect of entrepreneurship, including marketing, sales, promotion, client acquisition, and profits. Here are some ways to ground your practice/business:

  • Ground the space in which you conduct your Lightworking.

- Ground your checkbook, your bank account, your computer files, your Lightworking tools, and anything else associated with your practice/business.
- By using the power of your intention, you can add grounding elements to anything you create through your practice or business, including books, programs, courses, workshops, retreats, packages, card decks, etc.
- Ground the name of your business, the business entity itself, your website, and all of your social media and online groups.
- Ground your business and personal finances. Remember to re-ground after any significant expense, windfall, spending spree, etc.
- Ground yourself and your space before asking for the sale.
- Ground before any difficult conversation, like raising your rates, firing a client, delivering bad news, etc.

Here's a quick snapshot of some of the ways we each use grounding as Lightworkers. These lists are not meant as a guide for you to follow, but rather, to serve as examples of "the big picture" of grounding by two different real-life Lightworkers:

Amy:
- My work space is amazingly grounded, as I have intentionally selected artwork, crystals, colors, furnishings, accessories, scents, candles, and textures, and the room has been completely feng shui'd. I keep my workspace neat and orderly.
- I typically only work while I'm in my workspace. I don't conduct work in other parts of my home. If I need a break from my office, I go outside to ground.
- Before starting each block of client calls, I settle into my body and get still.

- I usually wear at least one piece of crystal jewelry or grounding jewelry every day.
- We don't wear shoes in our home, so I'm barefoot 75-80% of the day.
- I keep chocolate on hand when I'm writing. I set timers and I don't do anything except write until the timer goes off. If I become spacey or ungrounded while writing, I continue writing until the timer goes off, then I take a break and I leave my office to do something else for awhile.
- I make a to-do list every day to help me stay on track and prioritize but I do not stress about completing it all or not having enough time.
- I take breaks throughout the workday. I go outside, lie down in my bed or on the aforementioned Turkish rug, play a video game, daydream, take photos for my Instagram, stretch, go for a walk, or have tea. Ooooh what a glamorous life I lead, LOL.
- My intention every day is to finish my work before the kids are home from school, so I can be present with them in the evenings. Once I'm in bed for the night, I do NOT check email or do anything work-related.

Terry:
- I begin and end each day with a meditation filled with an intention of grounding, manifesting, healing, and gratitude.
- When I shower, I also hold the intention of grounding and healing the mind, body, and soul. Many talks are had with the Universe while in the shower.
- At least 2 to 3 times a week, I will go to the gym for me time because I gotta take care of the body my soul lives in.
- I am always barefoot while in the house but also take time to ground outside on the lawn while watching my lawn bunnies or out back while watching my

hummingbirds. Sometimes I will even go to the park and lay gazing at the sky.

- You will most likely see me wearing a bracelet that is made of copper, nickel, and brass to help with keeping my crazy energy at bay. I also wear labradorite and black obsidian.
- I make it a regular practice to go in the float pod, formerly called the deprivation chamber, for an hour at least once a month.
- I love hanging out in the Himalayan salt room as much as I can plus I have pyramid-shaped salt lamps in every room of the house.
- I have made it a regular practice to detox my body for 21 to 30 days through 100% juicing once or twice a year.
- When providing readings, I am always mindful to make sure I am connected and to disconnect afterward.
- With the nonstop busy schedule I seem to create, a balance of self-care is very important to me, so I make it a point to get acupuncture, massages, and pedicures regularly.

How much grounding do you need as a Lightworker? Well, how much sleep do you need? How much water does your body need? How much caffeine is too much caffeine? These are questions only you can answer. Feel free to refer back to the list of signs of being ungrounded from Chapter 1. If you're frequently having experiences from that list, or you're often tired or drained after Lightworking, then it's time to increase the amount of grounding you're getting. Don't worry about over-doing it. It's kind of like vitamin C. Most people are not getting nearly enough, and you really can't over-do it. Except, we're pretty sure extra grounding won't make your pee turn neon yellow. Dang, there's just no good segue to take us from bright yellow pee to Food for Thought, now is there? Oh well, here we go anyway!

Chapter 6 Food for Thought: please sir, I want some more

1. What are your favorite grounding methods so far? Which new methods would you like to try?

2. What's usually your first clue or indication that you're not grounded? On average, how long would you say it takes you to realize you're ungrounded and then resolve it by getting grounded? Can you think of at least one thing you could do or put in place to shorten this amount of time?

3. Have you had the experience of becoming ungrounded during a session as a Lightworker? How did you feel about the way you handled it then? If it were to happen again, how would you handle it this time?

Chapter 7:
When Grounding Isn't
Working

By now you may be feeling like a grounding rock star, empowered with a whole slew of grounding tools and techniques, perhaps with some you've even created yourself. But what happens when the grounding doesn't seem to be working? Never fear, there's an app for that. Wait, what? No, not an app, a solution. We meant to say there's a *solution* for that.

When the Grounding Won't "Stick"

As we've mentioned, grounding techniques tend to have an immediate effect. Therefore, you'll know right away if you implement a grounding method and it doesn't appear to be working. In some cases, this happens when a person or space refuses to ground.

For example, let's say that you grounded, and that grounding worked, as it always does, but then it was immediately undone, leaving you feeling ungrounded once again. This doesn't happen often, but it can be a bit unsettling when it does, so we want you to feel prepared and have some tools at the ready just in case.

Certain places are stubborn about grounding, which means the grounding won't "stick" and here are a few possible reasons why:

- **The space "underneath" the space is not grounded.** This could be due to ancient burial grounds, fracking, a "hanging space" like a deck or overhang, an old battleground, an underground water source or power lines, the site of a heinous crime years ago, etc. This doesn't mean the space can't be grounded, it just means it may require some specialty grounding. Remember how we talked about grounding a "hanging space" with a crystal grid? This would be effective and long-lasting, where simply intending the space to ground would feel short-lived. Likewise, battleground clearings take quite a bit of time and effort, and are definitely in need of "specialty" grounding. Ancient burial grounds typically need proper consecration before the space will feel grounded.

- **If one or more entities are hanging out in a space,** then a grounding won't "stick" until the entities are addressed and handled. That is a topic worthy of its own book as well. Check with either of us if you need assistance with these.

- **If there is an energy portal located in a space,** it will be very difficult if not impossible to ground the space while the portal is active. If you discover an energy portal and wish to have it relocated, contact a

Lightworker who is experienced in this area. Amy has handled these many times and can help you with this. She also cautions against attempting to "close" portals, as the benefits of this are typically frustratingly temporary.

- **If an ungrounded person resides in the space** or spends a significant amount of time in the space, it can be difficult to keep this space grounded. Some individuals refuse to ground. This can be intentional, as with someone who is attached to their pain or suffering, or lives in a "victim mentality" or a constant state of chaos, or it can be unintentional, due to issues such as mental illness or having numerous negative entities attached to their energetic field.

If you find you must spend time in a stubbornly ungrounded space or around such a person, the best thing you can do is ground yourself. And if possible, minimize your exposure to this place and/or individual. Use as many of the passive techniques as you can, to support all of your active grounding efforts. For example, wear jewelry that is grounding, wear grounding colors, scents, etc.

If you yourself feel energetically drained despite having performed substantial grounding work, we recommend checking your own field to see whether you have negative entities attached. You can refer to Amy's book *Pendulum Mojo* for specifics on Truth Testing, but essentially, you can use your pendulum to ask: "All things considered, do I have negative entities attached to my field?" And if you get yes, ask how many. Then you can use your preferred energy clearing/healing technique to remove those, or call on one of us to do it for you—we are both very experienced with this. Then use Truth Testing again afterward, to verify you've cleared them all. After that, your fatigue should resolve and your grounding will likely "stick."

Lightworking, Grounding, and Difficult Clients

What if this person who won't stay grounded is your client? Ruh-roh. At some point in a Lightworker's career, he or she will likely take on at least one client considered "difficult." We have certainly had our share of these as well.

For starters, it's helpful to consider that this person isn't trying to be difficult. This the only way they know how to be, and it's likely part of the reason they were drawn to you for help as their Lightworker. They are here because they do in fact require your help.

Secondly, *you* attracted this client, at this time, for some specific reason. You manifested this relationship and this exchange, perhaps to learn an important lesson, or to grow your capacity for patience and compassion, or maybe you just love a challenge. It's possible that you even knew they were going to be difficult before you took them on as a client, but you threw bleach on the red flags because you felt you needed the money, or you were excited to sign a new client— any new client. If that's the case, you're certainly not the first Lightworker to do that! Nor will you be the last.

And finally, working with ungrounded clients is a challenge that will require you to step up your game in order to be an effective coach, healer, or Lightworker. This is a true opportunity for your growth, and to expand the degree to which you can serve others. Creating a success story with this client will boost your confidence, make you better equipped to handle other clients, and help you clarify your ideal client through contrast. It will also push you to up your own grounding game, as you will need to ensure you are fully grounded when interacting with this ungrounded client.

If after you begin working with someone, you realize they aren't merely ungrounded, but *toxic,* then that's a horse of a different color. This can prove to be quite a predicament for a Lightworker, especially given that as a general rule, Lightworkers just want to help and don't like to disappoint people. Plus we tend to avoid confrontation and we suck at boundaries. The ability to set and keep boundaries is something both of us have worked hard to cultivate, and to help other Lightworkers instill in themselves. But what's a Lightworker to do if he or she finds himself or herself in a Lightworking commitment to an individual who is now known to be toxic?

Consider your options:

1. **Complete the existing agreement/package, but then do not invite them to re-up.** If they ask to keep working with you, our recommendation is to be honest but not brutally so. A toxic person is like a powder keg so you don't want to go sending off sparks. Rather than saying, "You are batcrap crazy so go bark up someone else's tree," you might consider saying something like, "It doesn't feel optimal for you to continue on with me, but I'm certain you will find the right Lightworker to pick up where we left off." Then it is imperative that you stick to that boundary and not engage any further with them. The crazier they are, the more they will try to sway you so be strong, stay grounded, and stand your ground!

2. **Make a request to terminate the agreement early.** If you choose this route, be certain you have carefully reviewed the terms of your agreement to ensure you're not in breach of contract. You do have an agreement for all your clients who purchase a package with you, don't you? If not, go through your notes and emails to see the specific terms of the arrangement. Because the only thing worse than being stuck with a toxic client is getting sued by one. You should also be prepared to

offer to refund all or a prorated portion of what they paid you. Err on the side of generosity, especially if the written agreement doesn't offer you a clear and specific "out." It's a good idea to consult an attorney before you make this request, because you just never know what a toxic person will do or what will set them off. Again, you'll want to keep it simple and direct, but not inflammatory. Check with your attorney to see if it's appropriate to use language like, "I'm not sure I'm the best fit to continue helping you with this issue. I'd like to refund your package fee so that you can find a more suitable coach/mentor/etc. to assist you with this."

3. **Address the issue directly with the intention of healing it.** This option is by far the trickiest and has backfired on Amy exactly three times. The first time it happened was many years ago because the then-newbie Spiritual Ass Kicker thought she could "fix" this person and made an Ego driven approach. Yeah, how often does that pan out? Years later, the second time it happened was because in Amy's eagerness to be of service, she didn't check in to see whether the person's toxicity was *optimal* to clear. Oops. The third time it happened, it was Spirit driven, and it was optimal to proceed, but the person's resistance was too strong. That time around, it was simply Amy's role to take a stand for this person, and then be the punching bag. Hey, sometimes you're the windshield, and sometimes you're the bug. If you choose this option, be sure you're not coming from a place of Ego, check in to ensure it's optimal, choose your words wisely, and release attachment to the outcome. And then let us know how it goes.

Naturally, the best solution in this case would be *prevention*. When it comes to taking on new clients, trust your intuition, don't ignore warning signs, and avoid making Lightworker decisions from your Ego... or your checking account balance.

Lightworker Trades and Barters

In the prior chapter, we mentioned the importance of having an even exchange of energy. This may or may not involve money, and a lot of Lightworkers start out offering their services for free, in exchange for gaining practice, and hopefully receiving constructive feedback. Some Lightworkers then choose to move on to a barter, to help ease them into the transition of fully valuing their abilities and ultimately, charging money for their talents.

As mentioned earlier, there is a big difference between giving freely and generously of your time and talents vs. being a doormat or being a person who doesn't value their gifts. An even exchange of energy creates balance, is grounded, and creates sustainability in the relationship.

Amy Scott Grant: Grounding Every Exchange

People have asked me to barter my services for everything from dance lessons and extracurricular activities for the kids to haircuts, Pilates, physical and energy healing, and more. I love barters because when they're set up properly, they can be just as satisfying and mutually beneficial as the more customary exchange of dollars.

When it comes to grounding, I treat barters and trades the same way I treat clients who pay cash. With my regular cash clients, we clarify expectations before we begin, and we sign an agreement that details those expectations, and then we carry out the terms of that agreement. But I have noticed that many people do not take this same care and attention when bartering for services. When I decide to enter into a trade for services with someone, I always start by saying, "If we're going to trade, then we must agree on this right now: if at any point our trade starts to feel unfair, then we will speak up and restore balance and equality by communicating." It's remarkable how many issues can be resolved through open communication, isn't it?

Once that is agreed upon by both parties, we then discuss and agree upon how we will balance the exchange. Some individuals I've bartered with have asked for a dollar for dollar value of exchange, while others have said, "Can you just do what I need here, and in exchange, I'll do whatever you need there?" Still others have requested an even exchange of time invested, hour for hour, regardless of our individual hourly rates. I'm not attached to the particulars of a trade, and I'm not looking to "get the best deal." When it comes to bartering, I'm more interested in whether or not I actually want/need what the other party is offering, and if that's a yes, then it comes down to what feels fair and balanced to me.

And if at some point in the future it starts to feel unbalanced, then I know I can speak up, because we've already agreed to resolve any imbalances through communication. Sometimes this is achieved by adding or subtracting contributions from one side; other times we agree it's best to dissolve the barter entirely. But by communicating, I find the relationships always remain intact, no matter the outcome of the trade. This is how I keep my barters feeling balanced and grounded.

Barters and trades can be wonderful, and we the authors have successfully employed these kinds of exchanges on several occasions. But what happens when a trade goes south? Lopsided exchanges can breed resentment, frustration, and eventually drive a wedge in the best of relationships.

Before entering into a trade, consider using Amy's approach to setting a ground rule for open communication. Be clear from the get-go about what each party is offering and what the expectations are. Whenever possible, clarify everything before the actual trade begins. And if a trade ultimately starts to sour, don't delay in your communication. This is not an issue that will resolve on its own, and the longer you wait, the harder it will be to broach the subject. Remember: your very relationship is at stake here. Isn't it worth a moment of discomfort to speak up and save it?

Remember to ground before initiating conversations or agreements about barters, and take time to ground the trade itself. You're sure to be glad you did.

Now are you ready for your final Food for Thought in this book? Let's go!

Chapter 7 Food for Thought: did someone say dessert?

1. Do you know of a person or place you would consider "stubbornly ungrounded?" After reading this chapter, what do you feel is your best strategy in handing this, going forward?

2. On a scale of 1-10 with one being not at all and ten being easy as pie, how easy is it for you to speak up when you feel ungrounded or out of balance in a relationship? How do you feel about your answer? Which of the grounding methods you've learned in this book do you feel will be most helpful in addressing these situations with greater ease?

3. What systems or processes can you put into place to help you avoid taking on toxic or stubbornly ungrounded new clients? How do you feel about employing these tactics?

4. Now is a good time to take a few minutes to add some grounding reminders into your calendar. How often, you ask? Good question. How often would you like to feel calm, cool, and collected? How often do you come unglued or feel stressed? Daily? Couple times a week? Maybe once or twice a

month? There's your answer as to how often you should remind yourself to ground.

If you have a digital calendar, schedule a recurring event as a reminder and you'll be good to go. Maybe you'll also want to shop for a cozy brown or deep red blankie, too. That way, we'll have something comfy to cuddle up with when we come visit you.

Conclusion

Congratulations! Now you know about a zillion (give or take some number just shy of a zillion) ways to ground yourself and others, what's next?

Here are a few issues/questions that may arise, now that you're a grounding maven:

- You will rapidly notice when people around you are not grounded. If you're grounded and they're not, just being around them may make you feel edgy or uncomfortable, like you can't wait to get away from the person. The reason for this is because you subconsciously fear you'll become ungrounded if you remain in their presence for too long. Truth be told, you just might. But now that you're aware of this, you'll be able to ground yourself in their presence.

- You may wonder what to do when you encounter someone who is not grounded. Are you really going to say to that Radio Shack employee, "Wow, dude. You should seriously ground yourself right now. In any zip code. And you don't need batteries for it."

- The decision whether or not to say something to an ungrounded person about their ungroundedness depends on a few factors such as who the person is, how they relate to you, the situation, the circumstances, the timing, how well you know this person, etc. But ultimately, the best thing you can do is check in with Truth Testing and see whether or not it's optimal to say anything.

- The best thing you can do when you encounter an ungrounded person is to ground yourself immediately. It's not just about the whole plank-in-your-neighbor's-eye principle, either. Grounding yourself will help you keep your cool about the situation, and make you less likely to get sucked into the other person's drama.

- How often should you ground? You already know the answer to that question, remember? As often as you need to. That will depend on you and what's going on in your life at that moment and sometimes, who you're hanging out with.

- You may start to notice weird things naturally grounded people do. For example, at a conference or multi-day meeting, they tend to choose a different seat every day. This pisses off the people who don't like change and those who thought they had dibs on the seat they occupied yesterday. The naturally grounded person is not trying to piss anyone off or encroach on someone's space; it's just that they may appreciate a change of scenery and/or get bored sitting in the same place next to the same people each day. Or perhaps they got here before you today and since you got the good seat yesterday, they think it's only fair to take turns. Or maybe they're trying to get away from someone who is clearly ungrounded. A woman once gave Amy the stink eye for an entire two-hour meeting because apparently "Amy took her spot." Unfortunately, this incident predated the show *Big Bang Theory,* so Amy couldn't start calling her Sheldon, which the woman certainly would have found hilarious. Yes, Sheldon, *that* was sarcasm.

- It's up to you to do what you need to do to get grounded. Don't wait for someone else to ground you. This might entail a nightly ritual before bed, or the need to unpack all of your clothes and toiletries the moment you arrive in a hotel room, or perhaps you'll need to request a different seat on an airplane, at a dinner party, or during a meeting. Don't drive off in that rental car until the mirrors, the steering wheel, and the seat are adjusted just how you like 'em. You are responsible for your own well being, and that includes grounding. Hopefully we've given you enough tools for your arsenal, so that you can quickly and easily ground in any situation.

- Cultivate compassion for people who are easily ungrounded. It's a stressful way to live. Better yet, why not gift them a copy of this book?

- Is there such a thing as being too grounded? No, there's not. If you meet someone who appears to be "too grounded," you might describe him or her as risk averse, afraid to lose control, afraid of failing, or unwilling to explore and experiment. However, these issues are not related to over-grounding, since there's really no such thing, especially for Lightworkers and empaths. The person who avoids any and all risk is not grounded and is paralyzed by their own fear. Being grounded means you are centered and clear, and free to evaluate risk appropriately. If you never risk, it's because your root chakra—and likely, other chakras as well—are blocked, which is a contraindication of being grounded. So ground away, because you can't overdo it! But please don't neglect your other chakras in the meantime.

Remember to seek progress over perfection. The goal is *not* to avoid becoming ungrounded at all costs; the goal is to swiftly notice when you are not grounded and restore yourself to a stable state of groundedness. Whenever you feel scared, overwhelmed, or stressed out, first take a moment to ground, and then you will have access to clarity to know what to do next.

Terry Robnett: Grounding with Hugs

Oh my gosh, hugs are THE BEST! They are a super form of grounding. If I get to boast, it is for sure about my hugging skills. Well, it's more like a gift, but I got mad hugging skillz! Ask Amy 'cuz ya know you can AskAmyAnything.com right? Did you know that hugging is very healing? I can't tell you how many times I have literally grabbed a person who I noticed was having a bad day and just hugged the crap out of them (despite some resistance) and they would thank me afterwards, admitting that they felt much better and that they really needed that.

My hugs can go on forever because I am always the last to let go. And when I hug, I get up in there and firmly squeeze with intent, love, and meaning. More often than not, it is as if the person I am hugging is hyped at a level 10 and the act of hugging them has brought them down to zero on a scale of 0-10. If this is not an example of grounding, then I don't know what is. Try it sometime. You might like it. In fact, you will probably love it because you will see all the miracles that comes from it. I have to say though, that it drives me crazy when I see people side hugging or doing one of those lame cheek to cheek hugs. What the hell is that? If you're gonna hug somebody, then do it with intention! Press your heart against theirs and heal them with a genuine loving hug! I dare you! I double dog dare you. Enjoy the power of hugs.

Over time, grounding will likely become a habit for you. When it does, you will find you are able to face life's challenges with ease and grace. Cooler heads prevail, and you'll finally be among them. Unless you're a two-headed dragon, in which case you'll be doubly cool. Except for the part about the fiery breath. Wait, can dragons even read? Never mind. Either way, you shall prevail.

We have thoroughly enjoyed creating this book for you, and it is our sincerest hope that grounding will enrich your life and the lives of those around you, bringing you greater peace, joy, and happiness.

BLESSINGS. AND HUGS. LOTS OF HUGS.

Glossary of Terms

NOTE: *This glossary only references terms mentioned inside this book; it is not meant to be a comprehensive glossary for all of Lightworking.*

active grounding – earthing method that requires specific action

animal energy – the subtle energy, symbolism, and metaphysical meaning of creatures, which can be accessed by humans in order to embody certain attributes which may otherwise seem lacking

aromatherapy – a form of alternative healing that uses scents, such as essential oils, plants, or other aromatics as treatment

badassery – the act of doing anything like a boss

barter – to trade goods or services in lieu of cash payment

body work – a general term used to refer to any kind of physical treatment or healing

boundaries – parameters put into place for the purpose of protection and safety. May be physical, emotional, conditional, etc.

breath work – a general term used to refer to any kind of specific, intentional breathing

136

card reader – A Lightworker who receives and interprets guided information using a special deck of picture cards. See also: oracle cards, angel cards, tarot cards.

chakra – an energy center in the body

chakra balancing – a Lightworking method by which the subtle energy of the chakra centers is opened and cleared. This is helpful to remove stuck energy in one or more chakras, as well as to eliminate energy bottlenecks if a chakra is closed or not properly functioning.

chakra work – a general term referring to any Lightworking method designed to clear, open, and balance the energy of the chakras.

channel (verb) – the act of allowing an energetic being (perhaps one who has crossed over) to speak through you, using your body to channel a message through to the living

channel (noun) – one who channels.

chanting – the act of repeating a rhythmic or sing-song phrase, without accompanying music

check in – a term used by Lightworkers when they are accessing intuitive messages or verifying the truth or validity of a message. As in, "Let me check in around that and see what I get."

chiropractic – a form of alternative healing by which joints are manipulated either manually or through a device called an "activator" for treatment of a variety of conditions

cords of energy – thin strands of subtle energy that connect the fields of two or more beings. Also: energy cords.

clairaudience – the ability to receive intuitive messages and awareness by hearing (auditory), either out loud or in one's mind

claircognizance – the ability to receive intuitive messages and awareness through an inner knowing and awareness, not necessarily through one of the five senses

clairsentience – the ability to receive intuitive messages and awareness by feeling; the ability to feel subtle energies and the emotions of others. See also: empath

"the Clairs" – a Lightworker term used to refer to the various types of extrasensory perception. See also: clairvoyant, clairsentience, clairaudient, claircognizance.

clairvoyance – the ability to receive intuitive messages and awareness in a visual way, either with the eyes or in the mind's eye

clear (adjective) – able to understand fully; having clarity. Also, the state of being after energy work is complete. "By the end of the session, I was totally clear."

clear (verb) – to remove blocks, doubts, fears, or limiting beliefs by working with the subtle energies. "I'm really stuck around money right now. Can you clear me?"

clearing (noun) – an act of Lightworking by which an obstacle (block, doubt, fear, limiting belief, upsetting emotion, etc.) is removed energetically. "After the clearing, he smiled and felt hopeful for the first time in years."

clearing (verb) – the act of helping a person to get clear through Lightworking

coccyx – the tailbone; approximate location of the root or base chakra; hurts for weeks if you fall and bruise it!

color therapy – type of healing in which certain hues and colors are implemented in an intentional way. In the context of grounding, ruddy reds and warm earth tones are used as color therapy to facilitate grounding.

combination grounding – earthing process that includes active and passive methods

crown chakra – the energy center located at the top of the head (crown). Typically associated with a sense of connectedness to all things.

crystals - naturally occurring rocks and gemstones that contain inherent healing qualities

crystal elixir – a liquid prepared by soaking a crystal in ordinary water whereby the water takes on the healing attributes of the crystal(s) and the liquid can then be used in healing work

divine – a word used by Lightworkers as another word for God. See also Source, Spirit, Highest Good, and Universal Energy

doubt – uncertainty

dowsing – refers to any type of divination that accesses subtle energies to "point" to an answer, such as pendulums, divining rods, or a forked stick used to locate underground water

dream board – visual representation of images and words suggestive of one's goals and intentions, designed to aid manifestation. Also: vision board

earthing – to become centered or well-balanced by connecting to the energy of our planet. Also: grounding

Ego – in Lightworking terms, the Ego refers to the aspect of self that seeks self-preservation and the avoidance of pain. Different Lightworkers have different perspectives on Ego, ranging from those who consider it our greatest ally, to those who feel it stymies forward growth and awareness. It likes to be capitalized. No surprise, right?

empath – a person who senses and deeply feels the emotions and sensations of other people and sometimes also knows another person's thoughts. See also: HSP.

empathetic – the ability to sense and deeply feel the emotions and sensations of others

empathic – See: empathetic

energy cords – See: cords of energy

energy exchange – the act of swapping value for value. In order for Lightworkers to remain grounded, it's helpful for them to create an even energy exchange for their services, either by receiving a payment or some type of barter involving goods and services.

energy field – general term used to describe the subtle energies of an individual person, place, or living being.

energy healer – a person who conducts energy healings

energy healing – a general term that includes any form of Lightworking designed to restore a person to a state of natural balance, which may be physical, emotional, mental, or otherwise.

energy portal – gateway for energetic beings to enter and exit the physical plane

energy vampire – an individual who demonstrates the tendency to suck the very life force from those around them

energy work – a general term that includes any form of Lightworking that interacts with the subtle energies

energy worker – a person who performs energy work

entity – an energetic being, usually without a physical form or body

etheric weaver – a special healing tool that resembles a large wire-wrapped crystal pendulum. It is said to embody the healing power of the Buddha Maitreya.

feng shui – meaning "wind water," this term refers to the ancient Chinese practice of arranging items within a space in order to create harmony

field – in Lightworking, this term refers to a person's entire area of subtle energy, which may include past, present, and future events. "I used my intuition to remove an entity from his field." Also: energy field

Gaia – another name for the planet Earth. Also: Mother Gaia

get grounded – process by which one connects to earth energy to feel more stable and centered

grounding – to become centered or well-balanced by connecting to the energy of our planet. Also: earthing.

grounding cord – invisible cord of subtle energy designed to help an individual connect to the energy of the earth

grounding energy – the stable subtle energies of the Earth

grounding mat – an earthing tool that one can sit, stand, or lie down on, or place under a chair or bed to (allegedly) facilitate connection to earth energy

grounding stone – a soothing crystal with properties of the earth, specifically used to facilitate earthing. Also: worry stone

group work – general term used to encompass Lightworking activities performed in groups of three or more. May include retreats, workshops, group sessions, etc.

Ha breathing – a rhythmic style of breathing that requires consciously counted breaths. Also: Huna breathing or Huna Ha breathing.

hanging area – in the context of grounding, this term refers to an area that exists as an overhang, without a solid foundation or structure immediately beneath it. For example, a second story deck, lanai, garage apartment, etc. Also: hanging space

Highest Good – a general term used by Lightworkers to refer to the best interest of all parties involved. "We stopped the treatment, because it was no longer in her Highest Good to continue."

Highly Sensitive Person (HSP) – term used to describe an individual who has SPS (Sensory Processing Sensitivity). These individuals are often deeply affected by strong smells, sounds, feelings, etc. A number of Lightworkers and empaths consider themselves to be HSPs. Also: HSP

Himalayan salt lamp – a soft glowing lamp fashioned out of a chunk of pink salt from Himalaya, said to have healing and energy cleansing properties.

HSP (Highly Sensitive Person) – term used to describe an individual who has SPS (Sensory Processing Sensitivity). These individuals are often deeply affected by strong smells, sounds, feelings, etc. A number of Lightworkers and empaths consider themselves to be HSPs.

Human Design – a map of human consciousness combining ancient wisdom of astrology, the Kaballah, the chakra system, and the I Ching. Provides deeper understanding of an individual's unique attributes (overt and hidden).

Huna breathing – a rhythmic style of breathing that requires consciously counted breaths. Also: Ha breathing or Huna Ha breathing.

intention – a specific thought, aim, or plan

intuition – an inner knowing or awareness

intuitive (adjective) – possessing an inner knowing or awareness

intuitive (noun) – a person who possesses an inner knowing or awareness

intuitive hit – a term used by Lightworkers to describe a flash of knowing. "I got an intuitive hit to turn left, so I followed it."

Lightworker - one who works with energy toward a positive end

Lightworking – a catchall term referring to any kind of intuitive or energy work

manifest – a term used by Lightworkers to refer to the process of intentionally or unintentionally creating

massage therapist – an individual trained and licensed in the art and science of manipulating soft body tissues for the purpose of relaxation and healing

meditation – the act of remaining still and focused for a length of time, for the purpose of quieting the mind, receiving intuitive messages, or relaxation

metaphysics – an abstract principle of philosophy that deals with intangible concepts like time, space, intuition, awareness, etc.

method – a specific way in which Lightworking is conducted

Mother Gaia – another name for the planet Earth. Also: Gaia

naturally grounded – a term used to describe an individual who stabilizes their own energy without consciously needing to do so

negative entity – an energy being that proves especially difficult or disruptive. "I didn't break that plate. It must have been a negative entity."

oracle cards – a divination tool consisting of a deck of cards featuring assorted imagery (and potentially also words and/or numbers). These are cards used to obtain intuitive insight or guidance for a person or around a specific question or issue. See also: angel cards, tarot cards

passive grounding – method of earthing that is "set it and forget it," without requiring ongoing action

past life – a person's prior existence as a physical being

pendulum – a weighted object that can swing freely on a string or chain. In Lightworking, a tool for dowsing and ascertaining truth.

protection – in Lightworking, a term that refers to any number of methods intended to prevent present or future harm

psychic (adjective) – possessing the ability to know information intuitively, or through means other than the five senses or the memory

psychic (noun) – a person who possesses psychic abilities

Reiki – a healing modality by which a practitioner channels life force energy and then transfers it to another being, usually through touch

Reiki master – a person who has achieved the Master level of Reiki attunement

remote – in Lightworking, this term refers to healing or energy work that is performed remotely, without being in each other's physical presence

resistance – the energy a person exerts in order to avoid facing some certain Truth about themselves; a refusal to accept

salt bath, also Epsom soak or Epsom bath – a healing treatment during which quality salts (preferably pink, gray, Epsom, Himalayan, or Dead Sea) are added to bath water to detoxify the body and cleanse the energy field

self-trust - one's ability to value, rely on, listen to, and believe in oneself.

shpritz – Yiddish term meaning spray. It just sounds better that "spritz," we don't know why.

Source (noun) – a word used by Lightworkers as another word for God. As in "the Source of all energy." See also Divine, Spirit, Highest Good, and Universal Energy

source (verb) – in Lightworking, this refers to the act of creating one's own healing methods or modalities. "I couldn't find anyone to fix this issue for me, so I sourced my own method and got it cleared."

Spirit – a word used by Lightworkers as another word for God. See also Divine, Source, Highest Good, and Universal Energy

spiritual healer – a Lightworker who restores balance to the subtle energies, clearing obstacles and effecting transformation

subtle energy – the realm in which Lightworkers operate, where life force is sensed in an intuitive fashion, rather than with the five physical senses

technique – in Lightworking, a specific method for accessing and/or affecting the subtle energies

third eye – the chakra located on the forehead, above and between the eyebrows. Typically associated with intuition and psychic awareness. Sometimes referred to as the "inner eye" or "mind's eye."

toning – the act of dragging out a single word or note for several counts

trade – to exchange goods or services in lieu of cash payment

truth testing – a process used to verify/validate information

Universal Energy – an expression used by Lightworkers as another word for God. See also Divine, Source, Spirit, Highest Good

146

vibe (noun) – short for vibration. In Lightworking, this refers to assessment of a particular vibration of subtle energy. "Dude, I got the weirdest vibe from that guy." Or, "I get such a good vibe from this apartment."

void – one of the five elements in Buddhism, related to stuff beyond the physical realm

worry stone – a crystal with properties of the earth, specifically used to facilitate grounding. Also: grounding stone

yoga – a form of body work that revolves around specific physical poses and a focus on the breath.

Resources

Amy Scott Grant's "Spiritual Ass Kicker" books, ebooks, audiobooks, and oracle cards are available on Amazon and on Amy's website:

http://AskAmyAnything.com

Pendulum Mojo: How to Use Truth Testing for Clarity, Confidence, and Peace of Mind

Spiritual Ass Kicker's Discovery Deck oracle cards

1-2-3 Clarity! Banish Your Blocks, Doubts, Fears, and Limiting Beliefs Like a Spiritual Badass

Patterns of Purpose: Color Your Way to a Better YOU

Spiritual Ass Kicker's Boom Book: Ignite Your Intentions and Create Blazing Results

Terry Robnett's books are available on Amazon:

Wealth Coloring Book: The Secret to Creating More Through Color

Love Coloring Book: Creating More Through Color

Happy Coloring Book: The Secret to Creating More Through Color

Terry's wellness products (such as Vitamin B12 energy patches and Vitamin D sunshine patches and liquid drops) are available on:

http://InnovativeBalance.com

The Lightworker's Guide to Getting Started is available on Amazon.

Schedule your Human Design session with Burry Foss to learn more about the person YOU were born to be!

http://askamyanything.com/humandesign

BRAND NEW!

Do you want help turning grounding into an easy and automatic habit?

Would you like to feel centered and connected all throughout your day, every day?

And would you like your life to feel more centered and steady?

Of course you would! Check out this special offer from the authors:

http://TheLightworkersGuide.com/groundme

About the Authors

AMY SCOTT GRANT

Thanks to her highly developed intuition and insatiable quest for human advancement, Spiritual Ass Kicker **Amy Scott Grant** has healed and helped tens of thousands of individuals in more than thirty countries through her speaking, writing, and mentoring. Her extraordinary gift of "Clarity with Hilarity" is no joke: results-based coaching + healing work peppered with a unique sense of humor and a healthy dose of levity.

In September 2013, Amy was inducted into the National Academy of Bestselling Authors and received a prestigious Quilly award at the Golden Gala Awards in Hollywood,

California. She was selected as a Thought Leader of the Year Finalist in 2013.

Amy has created a number of successful courses and digital products, including Ripple Magic, HIY (Heal It Yourself): Higher Power Tools, and MindTime™ meditations for kids at KidCentered.com. You can find Amy's writing all over the internet, as well as in the bestselling book *Inspired Marketing* by Dr. Joe Vitale and Craig Perrine; the acclaimed *Chicken Soup for the Soul: Life Lessons for Mastering the Law of Attraction;* the bestseller *Change Agents* with Brian Tracy; the bestseller *The Lightworker's Guide to Getting Started,* her *Spiritual Ass Kicker Series* (available on Amazon), and the forthcoming young adult novel, *Annabel the Lost.*

Ready to get clear? Connect with Amy directly and claim your free Spiritual Ass Kicker gifts at:

www.AskAmyAnything.com

About the Authors

TERRY ROBNETT, RN

Big strong hugs and hearty laughter are always on tap when you connect with **Terry Robnett.** She is a dynamic, powerful Lightworker, Reiki Master, and Registered Nurse (RN) with a heart of gold. Terry's unique blend of compassion and badassery make her a dynamo Consultant and Life Coach. She is passionate about helping you live into your full potential, so you can make a difference and make an impact.

Terry stands strong in her commitment to transformation, and her passion for health and well being is evident as she leads her clients toward a richer, more fulfilling life. She is the owner of Love-Healing-Balance as well as Innovative Balance, a revolutionary company created to help people take control of their health and wellbeing. Besides co-authoring the bestselling book *The Lightworker's Guide to Getting Started,* Terry is the author and creator of three manifesting coloring books: *Wealth, Love,* and *Happy.*

"Determination is born out of purpose... knowing that you are gifted for something and this something must be attained. It is never enough to rely on luck or natural talent. You must, above all, believe in yourself, face your goals, and then fight as if your life depended on it."

Discover your purpose and create change in your life now! Visit Terry's website and sign up for her FREE Daily Pumps guaranteed to make you smile:

www.LoveHealingBalance.com

Come Join Us in the

Lightworker's Guide

Community:

TheLightworkersGuide.com

It's free!

It's fabulous!

It's where YOU belong!

43017023R00091

Made in the USA
San Bernardino, CA
12 July 2019